PALACE *of* DECEPTION

ALSO BY DARRIN LUNDE

The Naturalist:
Theodore Roosevelt, A Lifetime of Exploration, and the Triumph of American Natural History

PALACE *of* DECEPTION

MUSEUM MEN *and the* RISE *of* SCIENTIFIC RACISM

Darrin Lunde

W. W. NORTON & COMPANY
Independent Publishers Since 1923

Printed in the United States of America
First Edition

All images courtesy of American Museum of Natural History

For information about special discounts for bulk purchases, please contact W. W. Norton Special Sales at specialsales@wwnorton.com or 800-233-4830

Manufacturing by Lake Book Manufacturing
Book design by Daniel Lagin
Production manager: Lauren Abbate

ISBN 978-1-324-06567-8

W. W. Norton & Company, Inc., 500 Fifth Avenue, New York, NY 10110
www.wwnorton.com

W. W. Norton & Company Ltd., 15 Carlisle Street, London W1D 3BS

1 2 3 4 5 6 7 8 9 0

For Sakura, Asahi, and Midori

CONTENTS

PART III
MAD DASHES

PALACE *of* DECEPTION

INTRODUCTION

Roy Chapman Andrews scanned the vast Gobi Desert. One by one he spied a number of promising rock outcrops on the horizon. The fossils were out there, he reassured himself, he just had to find them. With his wide-brimmed hat and holstered revolver, he was a man undaunted in his quest for adventure.

Standing beside Andrews in a stylish hunting jacket and pith helmet was Henry Fairfield Osborn, the president of the American Museum of Natural History. Desert sand swirled around him. It was 1923, and Osborn had joined Andrews on what he believed was the greatest fossil hunt in history. The New Conquest of Central Asia expedition was supposed to uncover Osborn's *Dawn Man*—the missing link to prove his belief that White Europeans had their origins on the high Asian plateau, far from the steaming jungles of Africa where Darwin thought humans evolved.

Greatly respected as a paleontologist, Osborn had the authority to make such claims. He had studied mammalian evolution for years and believed their fossils revealed a certain truth—that species evolved along definite pathways, as if marching toward perfection. Osborn held that several lineages of ancient peoples had "radiated" outward from central Asia as the seeds of the "races of man." He believed that the most advanced of these ancient lineages had moved westward into northern Europe, where the harsh winters eliminated all but the most intelligent and industrious to forge a superior race called the Nordics. From the icy realms of northwest Europe, a select group of these Nordics then migrated to the New World, where the story of their evolution continued.

As a member of one of New York's wealthiest families, Osborn identified as one of these New World Nordics. To Osborn, humanity was a race-based social hierarchy, with the likes of himself at the top. He believed the racial distinctions between people had biological meaning, and that it was simply a matter of evolution that his own kind had championed over the so-called lesser races. To Osborn, race explained the hierarchical world in which he lived, and with the help of Roy Chapman Andrews, he hoped to prove the origin story of the Nordics by finding their ancestor—the *Dawn Man*—in the depths of the Gobi Desert.

But Roy Chapman Andrews was not the only dashing explorer Osborn was using to push his racist agenda. He had already recruited the intrepid naturalist and pioneering taxidermist Carl Akeley to fill his museum with moralizing nature dioramas. "Nature teaches law and order and respect for property," Osborn said. "If these people cannot go to the country, then the Museum must bring nature to the city." The "people" Osborn was referring to were new immigrants, who were landing in New York harbor by the boatload. More immigrants arrived in America in the first two decades of the twentieth century than at any other time in the nation's history—at peak more than a million per year. To Osborn, the very existence of White America was at stake, and telegraphing his fears, he warned of the eventual extinction of the White race and of its "insidious replacement" by people of "less noble character."

Henry Fairfield Osborn used the allure of men like Andrews and Akeley to convey his social messages, and he did so while rebranding the American Museum as a place of scientific adventure.

Anthropologists marched through the ruins of Mayan civilization, ornithologists sailed the South Seas collecting tropical birds, and paleontologists like Andrews sifted through the sands of the Gobi Desert for fossils. During Osborn's reign, the museum launched hundreds of scientific field expeditions—more than at any other time in its history—and filled its halls with artifacts. Osborn nurtured a romantic aura that greatly enhanced the museum's appeal, and the AMNH stood as a model for natural history museums everywhere. The nation's newspapers published regular features on the museum's expeditions, and the faces of Carl Akeley and Roy Chapman Andrews were familiar to many Americans. Hundreds of children wrote the museum each year asking to join an expedition, and the AMNH became a beacon of scientific adventure, but beneath it all was Osborn's agenda.

This romantic era of exploration peaked in the 1920s, yet for many decades afterward, the allure of scientific conquest still held power. Long after their glory days, Akeley and Andrews remained the archetypes of swashbuckling museum adventurers, and they inspired many to follow in their path. It was this same aura that drew me to my own career at the American Museum in the early 1990s. I had always wanted to be a museum man of the Carl Akeley sort, and like one of those boys writing to Roy Chapman Andrews in the Jazz Age, I was drawn to the same spirit of adventure more than a half century later.

In common with Andrews and Akeley, I saw the American Museum as a place where I might express my interest in hunting and taxidermy, and I dreamed of joining expeditions to help fill the museum with treasure. Things were definitely different in the early 1990s: As a prospective employee, I was interviewed as much about my experience with firearms and taxidermy as I was about my knowledge of mammals and science. And shortly after I was hired, I was sent off on the first of many expeditions to hunt down new mammal specimens in the field. This would *never* happen to a new employee today. Younger colleagues of mine show surprise when I tell them of how I used to go off on far-flung expeditions to the Amazon, Africa, or the jungles of Southeast Asia. They are incredulous when I tell them of how I often carried a shotgun—and sometimes even a revolver—while living in the forest for weeks and months at a time. They find it hard to believe that I shot and trapped hundreds of animals in the field, and that I used my skills as a mammalogist and taxidermist to prepare them as museum specimens. Natural history museums are very different today, and the days of the hunter-naturalist are long gone.

Different though they might have been, I will always cherish my earliest experiences at the American Museum, and the steady rhythm of going off on expeditions—to the mountains of Peru, or the darkest lowlands of the Congo rainforest. I have spent years of my life living out of tents in some of the least explored parts of the world, and these experiences have allowed me to read the accounts of my museum predecessors with a knowing perspective. I lived a life that was reminiscent of what Carl Akeley and Roy Chapman Andrews experienced in their own romanticized age, and I loved it.

Historically, museums launched expeditions to build up their collections, and the American Museum certainly filled its storerooms with zoological treasures. There are vaults full of hippopotamus skulls, drawers of obscure New Guinea marsupials, and creaky vats of alcohol with partly dissected gorillas inside. Nearly all the specimens that Akeley and Andrews collected are still present in the museum. Kept behind the scenes, they are a library of the diversity of life on Earth.

Working with so many thousands of dead and preserved animal specimens is not for everyone, but I was drawn to it, and I can attribute my interest to having been raised within the bounds of nature-devoid New York City. Living in the city, nature always seemed so far away, but I compensated for this deficiency by building my own natural history museum—much of it composed of local specimens I'd collected and prepared. One nice thing about preserved animals is that they never run away. Carefully arranged in a drawer or on a shelf, they can survive unchanged for centuries. Museum specimens are forever accessible, and as a youngster in New York, that was what mattered to me.

Growing up in the 1970s and 1980s, I was often found scouring the streets for road-killed squirrels or rats, and after secreting these back to my room, I used them to teach myself a primitive form of taxidermy. Trips to the countryside were like expeditions in that they offered a chance at getting more exotic species, such as deer skulls or whole snakes. I was obsessed with collecting natural history specimens, if only to remind myself that there was a living world of nature just beyond the city. Museum specimens were my talismans, and like magic, they had the power to transport me to faraway worlds so filled with the possibility of adventure.

By about the age of fourteen I had amassed a serious natural history collection comprising a few hundred birds, mammals, fish, reptiles, and amphibians. Like a good curator, I kept a meticulous catalog of every one of my specimens. Paging through this old catalog today, and picking just one spread from 1986 at random, I can recall how, in the summer of that year, I carefully picked clean the skull of a pigeon that had been killed by a cat, and how I preserved the entirety of a catfish by plopping it into an old tomato sauce jar full of isopropyl rubbing alcohol. That same year I started setting mousetraps outside so that I could practice making museum study skins out of the rodents I caught, and I catalogued their skulls, too.

Perhaps I wasn't quite right in the head, but these are just a few examples of the many vertebrate specimens I collected, tagged, and dutifully preserved as a youthful curator. In truth, I was only mimicking the work of a museum curator, but keeping up with my boyhood museum served the purpose of firing my ambition to someday work for a real museum of natural history. There was a naïveté in my romanticized view of museums, but my youthful dedication was not for naught. I soon found myself employed at a very real natural history museum, and I have since spent my entire adult lifetime working for the largest natural history museums in the world—the American Museum of Natural History and the Smithsonian Institution.

Since joining these museums, expeditions have always been a big part of my work, and for the past thirty-five years I have either led or joined specimen collecting trips around the world. During these expeditions I collected thousands of mammal specimens while camped out in remote areas for extended periods of time. Many of these specimens are still being studied by scientists today, and a few were even put on exhibit. The reality, though, is that most people viewing these specimens have little sense of the strenuous efforts necessary to make these scientific collections a reality. Museum collections are built from the steady accumulation of specimens from hundreds of expeditions spanning many decades. For example, Andrews was responsible for collecting several thousand animals for the collections of the AMNH's Department of Mammalogy—everything from the skulls of Korean mice to complete skeletons of North Atlantic right whales. And yet his specimens represent just a tiny fraction of the hundreds of thousands of specimens currently housed in the AMNH.

Carl Akeley collected far fewer specimens in total, but he put them to more dramatic effect in exhibits featuring taxidermy animals. His works rank among the museum's greatest treasures, and I often made a special point to exit the museum each evening by way of Akeley's Africa Hall, if only to experience its undiminishing majesty. Working at the American Museum of Natural History, I found these two explorers and their contributions impossible to ignore, though the same could not be true for Osborn—a figure who always seemed to be lurking in the shadows.

Henry Fairfield Osborn challenged my perspective on everything. He was easy to overlook because he spent so little time on expeditions himself, yet he was the force that set the tone for the American Museum through its most influential years. Gazing out across

Central Park from his palatial corner office, he used the romance of adventure to foment White anxieties about race and human origins already simmering in his time. Heroic explorers like Andrews and Akeley were Osborn's emissaries, but beneath the glory of their expeditions were insidious racial underpinnings. *Palace of Deception* tells of the adventures of two of the American Museum's most famous explorers while at the same time putting the racial fears and anxieties that helped underwrite their journeys in sharp focus.

As president of the American Museum of Natural History (1908–1933), Osborn was considered an authority on everything from paleontology and evolution to race and eugenics. Having given *Tyrannosaurus rex* its name, he was a tyrant king himself. He believed in a hierarchy of races and developed his own theory of human evolution to challenge the randomness of natural selection. He presided over eugenicist meetings at the American Museum, and argued for the selective breeding of humans "even if the individual must suffer." He used his clout to sway politicians to support the Immigration Act of 1924, all but stopping the arrival of new Americans. Frustrated with what he called the "one-sided reports in the American press," Osborn visited Germany after the Nazis came to power in 1933 and pronounced himself "greatly impressed."

An imperious man well aware of his eminence, he required museum employees to vacate the elevator anytime he wished to ride it. Unbearably arrogant, he often spoke of himself in the third person—*Osborn will smoke his pipe now*—and on holidays he bragged of retiring to the family castle overlooking the Hudson River. The "romance of natural history" was Osborn's thing. He disliked the word "scientist," thinking "naturalist" had a nicer ring. He belonged to the circle of New York's wealthiest elites—J. P. Morgan was a favorite uncle, and Theodore Roosevelt a lifelong friend—and they offered him their money and influence, believing his agenda the best means to preserving their traditional ideas about race, class, and society.

Osborn led the American Museum through its greatest expansion, putting his stamp on every expedition and exhibit. He actively sought the most talented explorers, artists, and scientists, and then used them to transmit his ideas. African mammal dioramas were supposed to moralize uncouth immigrants. Fossil-hunting expeditions to the Gobi Desert sought to prove Osborn's presupposition of the *Dawn Man*. For twenty-five years, Osborn plugged the romance of natural history, twisting science to uphold his own view of the world—a racial pyramid with Osborn at the top.

Osborn also cofounded the Bronx Zoo with Madison Grant, whose book, *The Passing of the Great Race*, got the attention of Adolf Hitler. In an excited fan letter, Hitler gushed, "The book is my bible." Full of warnings about the so-called endangered White race, Grant's book was just the sort of drivel Osborn would like. That the author was a prominent wildlife conservationist was not unusual—racism was common among American naturalists, whose methods for classifying animals and protecting endangered species were just as easily applied to humans. Far from a pariah, Osborn was seen as a progressive in his time, his agenda resonating with the majority of White Americans. In no small part, that resonance stemmed from Osborn's effective use of his museum's most celebrated explorers—Akeley and Andrews.

Akeley was a pioneering taxidermist who dreamed of building a magnificent Africa Hall full of elaborate dioramas—an idea that came to him as a vision after an elephant mauling on Mt. Kenya. To achieve his dream, he needed to kill hundreds of animals for taxidermy, but Akeley considered himself an artist, not a trophy hunter. Shooting gorillas on the slopes of the Congo's Virunga volcanoes, Akeley felt like a murderer. Racked with guilt, he helped create Africa's first national park to protect the mountain gorillas of the Virunga volcanoes. He detested those who bragged of their hunting prowess, and so he had his wife—an erstwhile teenage runaway named Delia—shoot the elephants he needed to avoid being seen as a bloodthirsty White hunter. Pure in his desire to memorialize the beauty of African wildlife, and seemingly unconcerned with matters of race and class, Akeley was nonetheless in unwitting service to Osborn's efforts to project power and moral values to America's new immigrants.

Andrews led the AMNH's so-called *New Conquest of Central Asia*, which sent fossil-hunting expeditions across Mongolia's Gobi Desert. Dubbed the "Missing Link" expeditions, Osborn bet they would prove his assumption that White humans originated in central Asia, not Africa. The expedition unearthed a treasure trove of fossils—including the first dinosaur eggs—but nothing to prove any of Osborn's assertions. Pushing to the edges of the Gobi Desert, Andrews was driven as much by a desire to feed his own fame as he was to prove Osborn's hypothesis. He was the poster child of Osborn's worldview, and their synergy projected the fiction of White racial superiority.

The heyday of museum expeditions climaxed through the roaring 1920s—an age when everyone seemed to be in a hurry. Nobody expected the good times to last, and *Palace of Deception* is about how all three main characters were engaged in a race against time to realize their ambitions—Andrews wanted to be a famous explorer, Akeley wished to create an artistic masterpiece, and Osborn wanted to achieve greatness, not just as a scientific thought leader but also as a savior to White society. Everything came to an end with the Great Crash, as the Great Depression was then called. Expeditions nearly ceased, and Osborn was ultimately forced out of the AMNH, having become something of a dinosaur himself, his own students ridiculing his pseudoscientific ideas in the end.

The golden years of museum expeditions—a span of time roughly between about 1890 and the onset of the second world war—filled the storerooms of natural history museums with treasure, and scientists have been studying and making good use of this bounty ever since. Yet behind it all are Osborn's pseudoscientific and White supremacist agendas, and the legacy of this period still taints our most beloved museums today.

Writing this book has helped me make better sense of my own involvement with museums. I came to know and understand Henry Fairfield Osborn well past the midpoint of my museum career, which to me seems too late. How could I have not known about Osborn all those years? In this sense, understanding Osborn is part of my own way of coming to terms with my lifetime in museums. Like Andrews and Akeley, I, too, am somewhat the product of Henry Fairfield Osborn, and so this book can be thought of as part of my knowing myself.

Understanding where natural history museums have come from is the key to ensuring their ultimate emergence as something positive for the future. As the repositories of the many artifacts and biological specimens that form the basis of our understanding of our world—everyone's world—natural history museums have a vital role to play in the future, and I believe that future will be bright. Natural history museums are treasure troves that can be used to solve some of the most pressing issues of our day—everything from climate change, wildlife conservation, and invasive species, to food security, emerging infectious diseases, pandemic preparedness, and more. Museum specimens are critical to our addressing all these issues moving forward, and they must be preserved for future use.

As someone who has spent a lifetime working for two of the greatest natural history museums in the world, I feel optimistic for the future. Natural history museums can today claim their rightful place as instruments for great good, even as they strive to rectify the wrongs of the past. Much more work remains to be done. As one museum colleague of mine has explained, *museums may be all about the past, but that does not mean we need to live in the past today.* It is my hope that this book will be seen as just one small part of the process of setting things right for the future.

PART I

MUSEUM MEN

CHAPTER ONE

Enter the King

On a cool November day in 1892, Henry Fairfield Osborn—a dashing young professor—approached the American Museum of Natural History. Tall and handsome, Osborn radiated self-confidence as he walked—not arrogance so much as a serene awareness of his belonging. He certainly looked like someone who might one day reign over the museum, with his center-parted hair and walrus mustache. Always fashionably dressed, and with very gracious manners, Osborn was the picture of a New York City gentleman—wealthy, educated, and privileged. He was a magnificent specimen of a man, and he knew it.

The exterior of the museum was looking pretty good, too. Its newly constructed Seventy-Seventh Street entryway had only recently opened, and the new addition more than doubled the museum in size. Built out of rough-hewn granite, and with a central archway framed by jutting turret towers, the new entrance looked like a fortress. But it was just the start of the museum's expansion, and before the end of the decade its imposing façade would span the block—from Central Park West to Columbus Avenue. Like a castle, the museum loomed over Manhattan's Upper West Side.

Stepping inside, Osborn entered an expansive white marble

gallery. Doric columns studded the perimeter walls, but the spaces between them were not yet filled with the busts of great scientists. The museum was still too new for such reverie. *Jumbo* and *Samson* were the biggest names in the museum that year, and with his heels clicking against the tile mosaic floor, Osborn might have gone looking for their skeletons—the largest African and Asian elephants to have set foot in the New World. Not quite a quarter century old, the American Museum was still in its formative years, but to Osborn, it already seemed destined for greatness.

Founded in 1869, the AMNH was the brainchild of Albert S. Bickmore, an erstwhile student of Louis Agassiz, at Harvard's Museum of Comparative Zoology. A famous Swiss naturalist, Agassiz had left his natal land in 1846 thinking he would spend a couple of years in the New World, but he never returned home. Instead, he became something of an apostle of natural history in America. He traveled the country lecturing and teaching the virtues of natural philosophy. Settling into a professorship at Harvard in 1847, he sought to bring the natural sciences to America.

Agassiz was not unusual for his time in seeing nature as a window into the mind of God, and although never an orthodox churchgoer, his science was infused with the presence of the divine. A natural history zealot, he looked upon museums as if they were places of worship, and he believed all creatures were the result of special creation.

But for all his reverence, Agassiz was not against making use of animals. To the contrary, he was a firm believer in the need to collect and amass vast treasure troves of natural history specimens. He argued that this was especially important in America, where so much of the flora and fauna remained unknown. He was a true believer in the importance of zoological collections, and it is largely because of Louis Agassiz that natural history museums took off in America.

Having visited many of the greatest museums in Europe, Agassiz was appalled by the scrappiness of the collections he encountered in America. Whether it was the Charleston Museum or the Boston

Society of Natural History, he saw their collections as little more than assortments of curiosities, and he was not alone in thinking this way. Other commentators thought America's museums "so full of worthless and trashy articles" as to be hardly worth a visit. One critic described the nation's best collections as no better than those "made by schoolboys."

Even the Smithsonian Institution—opened in the city of Washington under the leadership of Joseph Henry in 1846—offered little hope for a decent museum. Henry thought the new institution should be more of a research center, where scientists could conduct experiments and discuss ideas. He was adamant that the Smithsonian should not include a museum, believing that such collections were "more suited to a sideshow" than to the needs of scholarship. If there was one thing Joseph Henry believed in firmly, it was this—that the Smithsonian should not have to "amuse the citizens and visitors of Washington" with a museum.

Seemingly alone in his fervor, Agassiz had little choice but to build his own museum. "Without collections lectures will remain deficient," he informed the president of Harvard in 1848. Having a particular interest in marine life, Agassiz raided the fish markets of Boston for interesting specimens, sometimes buying as many as fifty fish a day. He also solicited specimens directly from the public, leveraging his cachet as an Old World scholar to tap amateur naturalists. Americans longed to be a part of something bigger than themselves, and they sent Agassiz specimens as a means of being connected to something great. Circulating instructional flyers on how to preserve specimens, Agassiz received thousands of animals in return. He amassed so many jars of fish in alcohol that they filled the basement of Harvard Hall. Inevitably, his collection became the nucleus for Harvard's Museum of Comparative Zoology, which opened in 1860.

Albert Bickmore—an eager young man with a passion for natural history—had heard about the Museum of Comparative Zoology, and he traveled from his hometown in Maine to Harvard, hoping to study under Agassiz. Arriving on campus, Bickmore found the professor in the basement of his museum, amidst the gloom of pickled animals. He approached cautiously. "I am looking for the professor," Bickmore said. "Dis is me," Agassiz responded, peering over some amber-colored jars. Agassiz was already sizing him up. He had a standard way of testing prospective students, and after later deciding on some sea urchin specimens, he challenged Bickmore to learn everything he could about the animal based on nothing more than the specimens in the jar. As Agassiz explained to him, "you will either become utterly weary of the task or else you will be so completely fascinated with it as to devote your whole life to the pursuit of our science."

As it turned out, Bickmore passed Agassiz's test, and became his star student. "Professor Agassiz was as wise an instructor as he was an able and successful investigator," he wrote of his mentor. To pay for his education, Bickmore worked in Agassiz's museum, where he was tasked with keeping the collections of starfish, urchins, and sea cucumbers. It was a mundane job, but he was soon promoted and put in charge of the museum's shell collection, which was something of a big deal. "I have made some progress towards 'getting up' in the museum, if not the world," Bickmore excitedly wrote his father, saying that he hoped his position at the museum might one day become permanent.

Absorbing Agassiz's enthusiasm, Bickmore grew ever more excited with his studies, each day in the museum bringing him further joy and enthusiasm for his chosen profession. When crates of new specimens arrived, Bickmore was always there to examine the contents as they were opened. "This work of unpacking is one of the most exciting and profitable of any we have at the museum," Bickmore wrote of the experience, knowing that each crate might hold something rare or completely unknown to science.

It was not long before Bickmore decided to found his own museum. He thought it was odd that Agassiz had established his Museum of

Comparative Zoology in the sleepy town of Cambridge, where donors were scarce, and not all that rich anyway. Bickmore thought he could do better, and he dreamed of founding his own museum in New York City, the very heart of America's wealth and power.

Not that New York lacked museums. Phineas Taylor Barnum had long run his so-called American Museum in downtown Manhattan, just across from City Hall. There Barnum displayed thousands of natural history specimens, including such exotics as orangutans, kangaroos, and live beluga whales. One of his more popular attractions was *The Happy Family*, a large enclosure filled with live predators and their prey—rabbits and weasels, hawks and mice, foxes and hens—all living peacefully together. *The Happy Family* became so well-known that it was used to describe President Lincoln's cabinet, in light of the intense rivalries known to exist within that body.

Full of both live and stuffed animals, Barnum's American Museum contained more natural history specimens than any other venue in New York City. In truth, his place was much more than a museum, being equal parts zoo, theater, and lecture hall. It also included a very sizable aquarium, and in the summer of 1862 the showman hired Bickmore, by then a competent marine biologist, to join a maritime expedition to Bermuda. Bickmore's job was to collect live tropical fish for Barnum's displays, and as a bonus, he was allowed to keep any extra specimens for his own studies. It was Bickmore's first experience on an expedition, and he was thrilled.

But Barnum was nothing more than a showman at heart, and his place was so full of humbugs, like his *Feejee Mermaid*—a monkey torso stitched to the back end of a fish—that it was an embarrassment to the more respectable classes. Worse than his so-called mermaids were his live human exhibits featuring bearded girls and so-called fat babies. Stoking racial fears in the run-up to the Civil War, Barnum abandoned all decorum with his *What is it?*—in truth a mentally disabled Black man dressed up in an ape suit and trained to act out the most savage fears of White society. Barnum gave museums a bad name. Indeed, Barnum had all but commandeered and debased the very meaning of the word *museum*. No wonder Joseph Henry wanted to avoid the same fate for the Smithsonian. Still, Bickmore believed that he could do better.

Fired with ambition, Bickmore made a detailed sketch of his imagined museum, carefully considering everything right down to its display cases, which he specified should be T-shaped to make the best use of available space. Carrying these plans folded and tucked inside his Bible, he pulled them out for anyone willing to listen to his idea. It was too bad the "Great Rebellion" got in the way of his plans. Bickmore had certainly followed news of the Civil War, and especially Lincoln's call for volunteers, but it was only after he returned from Bermuda that he learned that many of his classmates had already enlisted and joined the fight.

Feeling compelled to do something himself, Bickmore joined the Forty-Fourth Regiment Volunteers and was deployed to North Carolina, where he saw action during the Battle of Goldsboro Bridge, and was nearly killed when his regiment was pinned down by sharpshooters. In one close call, a split-rail fence stopped a bullet that would have otherwise gone clear through his head.

Bickmore was honorably discharged from the US Army before the end of the war, but he was restless, and despite all his previous enthusiasms, could not bring himself to go back to studying sea urchins in the basement of Agassiz's museum. He longed to join an expedition like the one he had made for Barnum, and with the excitement of being in the field still fresh in his mind, Bickmore shipped off to the East Indies. His stated goal was to make a collection of seashells for his future museum, but the trip turned into a two-year jaunt through Asia. Along the way, Bickmore survived fevers, tangled with an enormous python that had been given to him as a surprise gift, and nearly died when an earthquake sent him sliding into the caldera of a volcano. Fortunately, he was able to grab hold of a strong-rooted fern before falling into the abyss. Soon after returning to the

United States, in 1867, he published a narrative of his adventures—*Travels in the East Indian Archipelago.*

More than the beloved collection of seashells he had made along the way, Bickmore's travelogue helped him rally support for his planned museum. He was an excellent public speaker, and giving talks about his adventures helped him to get benefactors behind his cause. New Yorkers were especially eager to show off their wealth after the war, and with the help of Theodore Roosevelt Sr., Bickmore mustered a band of loyal supporters.

It also helped that there were two important European collections up for sale. One was the cabinet of Maximilian, Prince of Wied, who had traveled through Brazil and the American West in the early nineteenth century. The other was that of the late Monsieur Verreaux, a Paris taxidermist whose private collection included specimens from across the French empire. Taken together, these collections raised hopes among the future trustees that the nucleus of a natural history museum could be readily obtained, and they sent Daniel Giraud Elliot, an early museum supporter, across the ocean to Europe to broker some deals.

As plans for his new museum progressed, Bickmore still had to contend with Barnum's establishment downtown. The showman was notorious for undercutting emerging competition, but this problem was solved when a spectacular fire tore through Barnum's museum, sending performers and exotic animals fleeing into the streets. The destruction of Barnum's venue on March 2, 1868, led to a *New York Times* article that asked, "Why cannot we now have a great popular Museum in New York, without any 'humbug' about it?" The article continued: "In respect to this type of thing, our city is, and always has been, a marvel of poverty. Compared with any one of the hundred larger cities of Europe, we are beneath contempt."

At last, everything seemed set for Bickmore's museum to become a reality, and on April 8, 1869, the charter for the new American Museum of Natural History was signed in the front parlor of

Theodore Roosevelt Sr.'s home, whose namesake son would be the twenty-sixth American president. Among the nineteen men present at the East Twentieth Street residence were J. Pierpont Morgan, the financial titan, and Morris K. Jessup, a self-made railroad man whose formal education extended to only the sixth grade. All were united in their belief that the new museum would bring the city prestige while also uplifting the working classes and promoting social stability.

At first, the American Museum occupied borrowed space on the upper two floors of the Central Park Arsenal—an old munitions storage building near the menagerie on the southeast corner of the park. This was the most fashionable district in the city, and although Bickmore displayed his specimens with staid Old World formality, people still flocked to his exhibits. Everything seemed to be off to a great start, but the museum still needed a permanent home, and after much wrangling, the trustees agreed to move to an eighteen-acre plot on the Upper West Side called Manhattan Square.

Right away, Bickmore was leery of the new site. It was a wasteland of rocky crags and stagnant pools. All around there was nothing but dilapidated squatters' shanties and herds of grazing goats. The only new construction was the Dakota Apartment Building on Seventy-Second Street, so named because it might as well have been in the Dakota Territories, it was so remote. Most critically, the sole means of transportation to the area was an unreliable horsecar service that ran along Eighth Avenue. There was not yet any rail service, and people really had to go out of their way to reach the future museum site.

Bickmore's fears were allayed somewhat when he learned that Frederick Law Olmsted and Calvert Vaux—the architects of Central Park—would be preparing the site, and that Jacob Wrey Mould would design the museum building itself. These were respected architects, and as construction began in 1872, people started to donate specimens. Among the earliest acquisitions was a great auk, a penguin-like bird that had recently gone extinct. Less impressive were such oddments as a stuffed crocodile, blocks of granite, and a single vertebra from a long-dead whale. One early donation comprised "one bat, twelve mice, a turtle, four bird eggs, and the skull of a red squirrel" from a fourteen-year-old future president of the United States, Theodore Roosevelt. Stranger yet was a pickled human hand from Barnum—a specimen that continued to exist in the museum's collection for many decades, preserved in a somewhat leaky glass box of peppermint-scented oil.

By 1874 it was time to hold a cornerstone ceremony, and using a specially engraved trowel—an artifact now on display in the Smithsonian Institution—President Ulysses S. Grant slathered some mortar on the museum's bare foundation. Three years later, in 1877, the first museum building was complete, and all the specimens were moved up from the arsenal building. On the first floor, the museum displayed Bickmore's prized shells together with more than a thousand stuffed mammals and articulated skeletons from the recently purchased Maximilian and Verreaux collections. The second floor accommodated some ten thousand stuffed birds on pedestals, and on a gallery above, Native American artifacts. Finally, the fourth floor housed the fossils. Thus, the first building of the new American Museum was filled.

Early photographs of the museum show a building standing alone in the middle of an otherwise vacant lot of rocky rubble, yet inside and out, the building had an undeniable elegance, with its ornate tile floors, high ceilings, and oversized plate glass windows that let in an abundance of natural light. Of particular note were the gas light fixtures, which allowed the museum to extend its hours well into the night. One night, several weeks before its grand opening, Bickmore and his assistants illuminated every floor in the new building, making it visible from New Jersey, across the Hudson River.

Today, much of the building's original charm has been lost to the layers of modifications and renovations in the century and a half since its completion, but having occupied an office in one of the spacious "apartments" on the fifth floor of this original building, I once enjoyed an office with a spiral staircase leading to a wraparound mezzanine filled with Australian marsupial specimens. Viewed from the outside, the original AMNH building is now nearly entombed within a conglomeration of dozens of other buildings added through the years. At the time of this writing, the AMNH is just filling in what was practically the last bit of remaining building space on its northwest corner, and so the first building of the AMNH—Section One—is all but eclipsed from view except from the air.

In 1877, the new museum opened to great fanfare, with President Rutherford B. Hayes presiding as guest of honor. In a rousing speech he declared the American Museum of Natural History officially opened. Everything seemed to be going well until the very next morning, when Bickmore found the place almost deserted. The new museum building was so remote and inaccessible that even the trustees were reluctant to visit. "No matter how fine the exhibits are, if no one saw them what good are they?" one of them asked. Eventually, Morris K. Jessup, one of the museum's founding trustees, was given the task of fixing the situation, but optimism was scarce. One trustee wrote Jessup, urging him to "check the wild extravagance" of Bickmore, while another suggested that perhaps the museum should only be open a few days a week.

Bickmore had hoped to make the museum a center for scientific investigations, but with most of the trustees woefully ignorant of natural history, they lost interest fast. They had little idea of the value of science, and even less of a notion that research was a proper task for museums. Whereas all the great museums of Europe kept elaborate collections behind the scenes for scholars, the trustees of the American Museum, more practical men, believed the museum should only be concerned with educating the working classes, and perhaps providing them with a little "innocuous amusement."

Charged with finding a solution, beginning in the spring of 1880, Jessup visited the museum daily in order to observe the reactions of its visitors. At first, he was critical of the museum, fearing that

Bickmore and the curators had fallen into the habit of thinking the trustees would buy them any specimen they desired. Day after day, Jessup made the long trip to the AMNH, but the more he observed, the better he came to appreciate Bickmore's ambitions. The museum was an important gathering place for naturalists, and Jessup was impressed with their "devotion to their work and the museum."

Finally, when it came time for Jessup to report on his findings, to everyone's surprise he explained that if anything, the museum should be enlarged and expanded. "We ought to have more lions and other big animals because they are what interest the public the most," he wrote, adding that he felt the museum collections could be "a power for great good" in helping the citizenry understand the *moral lessons* that could be gleaned from nature. That natural history collections could convey morals to an otherwise ignorant public was a notion straight out of the teachings of Agassiz, and it was transmitted, through his student Bickmore, to Jessup. Suddenly, the trustees were awakened to the idea that museums could serve as important instruments for social indoctrination and control. That their institution could be so *useful* was something that really got the trustees' attention, and they now looked to Jessup for guidance on how best to expand the museum.

Among the things the public really wanted to *see* were primates. Ever since Darwin's publication of *On the Origin of Species* (1859) and *The Descent of Man* (1871), people had been fascinated with evolution and human ancestors. Museumgoers wanted to view apes and monkeys, if only to convince themselves that they were not descended from such creatures. Indeed, it was scientists who were among the most ardent skeptics of evolution. Agassiz in particular rejected Darwin's theory outright, and instead believed that God had specially created each species. "The resources of the Deity cannot be so meagre, that, in order to create a human being endowed with reason, he must change a monkey into a man," said Agassiz. Jessup, however, was not so sure, and he placed a standing order with Wards Natural Science

Establishment—the premier supplier of museum specimens—to acquire examples of every known species of primate in the world.

Jessup became the president of the museum in 1881, and there followed a dramatic expansion of the museum's activities. He added to the bird and mammal collections, realizing that these had always been the museum's chief attractions, and he enlarged the professional scientific staff. By 1885, Jessup decided that "perhaps the museum should begin to aid original research in a more active manner," and this led to the formation of a Department of Mammalogy and Ornithology, and the hiring of Joel Asaph Allen to oversee the museum's research program.

Allen was a fellow graduate of Agassiz's program at the Museum of Comparative Zoology, but unlike Bickmore, who was more of a dreamy romantic, Allen was a disciplined researcher. Soon after arriving at the museum, he discovered that both Bickmore and Jessup had little understanding of the needs of professional naturalists. True, the museum had acquired some important collections from the early nineteenth century, but these were hardly suited to the needs of a scientist on the cusp of the twentieth century.

Earlier in the century, naturalists were content with describing and classifying the many new species coming into museums. But later in the century—and especially after Darwin—naturalists were more interested in evolutionary questions. No longer content to just name and classify species, they wished to study the process of evolution itself. Museum specimens were still very relevant, but there needed to be many more of them, and from a greater variety of geographic areas for them to be useful. Whereas under the paradigm of special creation, one or two examples of a species might have been sufficient to represent each kind of animal, in the age of Darwin, thousands of specimens were needed to document their variation and evolution. As such, the late 1880s saw the museum's earliest organized collecting expeditions, the first of which was to Montana to obtain specimens of the dwindling American bison.

Allen also brought to the AMNH an awareness of America's nascent preservationist movement. The country was changing, and its scenic landscapes and abundant wildlife were under threat. Preservation was the word of the day, but in addition to wanting to save animals like the American bison, the movement attracted those who sought to preserve social norms, too. As a reaction to rapid modernization and social transformation in the late nineteenth century, the preservation movement emerged as much for saving scenery and wildlife as it did for preserving traditional ideals and values about race, class, and society, and it took early root in the AMNH.

Through the first decade of its existence in its new building on the Upper West Side of Manhattan, the AMNH went from being an institution struggling to find meaning to one dedicated to promoting moral lessons through the use of science. Museum specimens were the key, and in the 1890s the AMNH redoubled its efforts to build up its collections. As more and more specimens came in, the need for collections storage space became acute, and plans for an impressive new entry pavilion on Seventy-Seventh Street were put in motion.

This was the AMNH that Osborn saw in the fall of 1892 as he approached the new Seventy-Seventh Street entrance to the museum. Indeed, he was a very fine specimen of the "old stock" White American aristocracy, and he had good reason to feel self-assured that day. Osborn had only recently been hired as the museum's first curator of paleontology. What is more, he simultaneously became a professor of zoology at Columbia University, just uptown. The dual appointments came as no surprise because Osborn had spent months finagling the arrangement. Certainly, the museum wanted Osborn for his knowledge and ambition—there was no question he was qualified for the job—but they also wanted him for his money and family connections. More than a scientist, Osborn belonged to one of New York's wealthiest families, and that mattered.

To Osborn, the AMNH seemed perfectly tailored to his own

interests and objectives. He wished to study the fossils of extinct mammals, but more as a means to answering bigger questions about evolution. Although religious, Osborn had no qualms with the idea of evolution, and he was determined to discover new laws governing the origins of species. Not entirely convinced by Darwin's theory, he believed the museum's collections would inspire him to make an important discovery of his own. Indeed, Osborn saw Darwin as just the latest in a long line of evolutionary thinkers going all the way back to Aristotle, and as far as Osborn could tell, he himself had a very good chance of becoming the next great evolutionary thinker after Darwin.

Entering the American Museum of Natural History in the fall of 1892, Henry Fairfield Osborn was poised to simultaneously transform himself, the museum, and society.

CHAPTER TWO

Protestant Evolution

Henry Fairfield Osborn was born on August 8, 1857, into a world of plutocratic privilege. His father, William Henry Osborn (1820–1894), was a shipping magnate and railroad tycoon. A classic gilded age captain of industry, he was instrumental in making the Illinois railroad a financial success. Traveling often through the American West for his work, he had a practical approach to business, and soon instituted a program of actively recruiting German and Scandinavian immigrants so that he could deliberately settle them along his railroad lines. This scheme would prove very convenient because as these immigrants farmed the land and worked in new factories, they had little choice but to ship their goods east via Osborn's own railroads, making him rich.

Henry's mother, Virginia Reed Sturges (1830–1902), also came from railroad wealth. Her father actually owned the Illinois line that her husband so successfully managed, but she was hardly comfortable living a life of ease. A deeply religious woman raised Presbyterian, she devoted herself to serving God through self-sacrifice. "We would be poor, weak, delicate plants if only visited by prosperity," she said, believing her worldly deeds would pay dividends in the afterlife. Optimistic in her religion, she never fell into the gloomy belief that certain souls were predestined for damnation. Her adult son recalled how she followed the "lighter, happier and truly Christian side of religion, chiefly exemplified by good works, benevolence, and patriotism." Yet for all her upbeat religiosity, and her certainty of the afterlife, she was still haunted by death. "It is hard to believe that the young and happy can die," she confessed. "I say to myself I may too die?"

William and Virginia raised Henry to be both pious and ambitious. He grew up studying the Bible, and his daily life was filled with religious commitment. From his father, young Henry developed a businesslike work ethic that would serve him well in science, but he was more powerfully influenced by his mother. Admitting that Henry was "the child of her prayers," Virginia drilled her religious convictions into her son, and she shaped the spiritual framework upon which he would later scaffold other ideas about evolution, race, and society. She taught him to nurture his own personal relationship with God, and to struggle not just for material success but spiritual salvation as well. So great was his mother's influence, that for the rest of his life, Osborn never wavered in his belief in God.

As a young boy, Osborn lived with his family in a Manhattan town house at 32 Park Avenue, in the wealthiest district of the city. For a bucolic change of pace, the family spent summers in the Hudson Valley, where they had an estate in Garrison overlooking the river. Years later, the family would build an even grander home nearby, called Castle Rock. Set atop a promontory with spectacular views of the Hudson River across from West Point, Henry would one day reside here as the Osborn family patriarch.

Dividing their time between Manhattan and the Hudson Valley, the Osborns hobnobbed with New York's moneyed elites. They mixed easily with the Roosevelt and Vanderbilt families, and their social status peaked when Osborn's aunt married the financier J. P. Morgan. Although the marriage did not last—the newlywed Aunt Amelia died of tuberculosis soon after her wedding—Morgan remained a supportive uncle to Osborn for the rest of his life.

The family's wealth notwithstanding, Osborn was raised with the expectation that he strive beyond his social position to achieve something worthwhile all on his own. This was not some vague suggestion but a very real and constant pressure. Neither of his parents would have tolerated him living a life of moneyed ease, yet for much of his youth, Osborn had little notion of what he wanted to do. Unlike his older brother Frederick, who was a playmate of Theodore Roosevelt and fond of collecting natural history specimens, Henry had never shown any particular interests. He was just an ordinary child. It was only after he started attending Princeton College—and even then, only near the end of his junior year—that he discovered his calling.

Having just taken a refreshing swim with two of his classmates, Osborn was lazing on a grassy knoll above a canal. It was a hot June day and exams were nigh. The boys were trying to read Paley's *Natural Theology*—a book that extolled the virtues of finding God in nature—but they were more in the mood for talking. One of the boys, William Berryman Scott, mentioned reading an article in *Harper's Weekly* about some Yale students who joined their professor on a Western fossil-hunting expedition. The Yale College Expedition of 1870 was just the first of several Yale "bone hunts," but the Princeton boys were loath to let their Connecticut rivals dominate the field. "Why can't we do something like that?" someone said, and Osborn was sure that they could.

Up until that time, Osborn had been planning to join his father in the railroad business after graduation, but he was hardly looking forward to it. The prospect of a Western fossil hunt, however, was immensely exciting. At that time, the science of paleontology was in the hands of two personalities: professor Edward Drinker Cope (1840–1897) of Philadelphia and professor Othniel Charles Marsh (1831–1899) of the Yale Peabody Museum. Both men were independently wealthy, and there was an intense rivalry between the two that only grew more vicious with each passing year.

Their mutual hatred began when Cope botched the reconstruction of a fossil *Elasmosaurus* skeleton—a large marine reptile from the Late Cretaceous era. Cope had put the skull at the end of the animal's tail, thinking it was the neck. Marsh was quick to mock Cope's ignorance—he didn't know the head from the tail of an animal—and Cope had to scramble to retract copies of the research paper he had just published with the mistake so prominently illustrated. Marsh never let Cope live it down, and their rivalry only intensified as each tried to outdo the other by describing ever more spectacular fossils. Both men tapped their personal fortunes in order to find bigger and better fossils. Rushing to publish new results, Cope continued to blunder, while Marsh resorted to bullying and bribing fossil hunters to get the best specimens. Their published exchanges were filled with poisonous barbs, and their open hostility deterred many from entering the field.

None of this fazed the Princeton boys. They largely ignored the Cope-Marsh "bone wars," and while planning their Western trip, Osborn and Scott had innocently sought Marsh's advice on where to dig for fossils, but he refused to speak to them. When they went to visit Cope, he received them, but he was wary, thinking they were spies sent by Marsh. Asking Cope if he thought there might be any fossils in the Bridger Basin of Wyoming, he shot back—"Well, there were before I got there." Thus, America's most eminent paleontologists were not very encouraging. Still, Osborn and Scott managed to create sufficient momentum to launch the First Princeton Expedition in the summer of 1877.

Having just celebrated its centennial, the United States was in the thick of the Indian Wars. Crazy Horse and his warriors were defeated in Montana, and the United States soon afterward annexed the Black Hills from the Sioux, while at the same time driving Sitting Bull and his band of Lakota into Canada. The West was opening up, at least for

Whites, and dressed like cowboys, Osborn and a klatch of eighteen of his classmates set off on an adventure that took them through Colorado, Utah, and the Bridger Basin of Wyoming. Traveling on horseback, they were armed with rifles and revolvers provided by the US Army for protection against hostile Indians, a threat that never manifested. At first, the expedition floundered around Colorado, as William Berryman Scott later recalled—"Our little rats of mules were greatly overburdened and we had to store a ton or so of useless stuff at a friendly ranch. No plan of exploration had been made, no localities suitable for collecting had been fixed; in fact, the expedition threatened to deteriorate into an aimless wandering about."

Unprepared for high-altitude exposure, Osborn suffered agonizing sunburn. He insisted on wearing "a little felt hat, with only an inch or so of brim," Scott recalled, and his nose "never did stop peeling." Stopping at a mining camp in the mountains, an "old timer" there remarked to him: "Stranger, either you'll have to widen out that hat-brim, or else call in that nose." After weeks of aimless wandering through Colorado, which Scott described as "a wanton waste of time, money, and opportunity," the expedition hit pay dirt at Fort Bridger, Wyoming. Making camps in the surrounding badlands, they found their first vertebrate fossil—that of a little three-toed horse—and later excavated the skull of a massive *Uintatherium*—an extinct plant-eating mammal much akin to a rhinoceros.

Looking rather tanned and lean, Osborn returned from the expedition completely enthralled with paleontology. He was drawn to the romance of fossil hunting, and he waxed poetic when writing up the results of his expedition—"in these rocks are buried many generations of animals whose genealogy can often be clearly followed . . . the records of an ancient land are written in characters which cannot be mistaken." Suddenly, Osborn thought he might have a future as a scientist. He went back to Cope, who was more receptive now that he realized Osborn was not a spy, and seeing young Henry as a kindred spirt, he delighted in showing him his most treasured fossils.

Having found his calling, Osborn soon attracted the attentions of James McCosh, the president of Princeton College. A paleontologist himself, McCosh accepted the fact of evolution, but not as it was described by Darwin. This was during the time in history—roughly 1880–1920—that would later be called "the eclipse of Darwin" when evolution was widely accepted in scientific circles, but with very few conceding that natural selection was the primary mechanism. Darwin himself admitted that selection might not be the sole driving force behind evolution. Several possible alternatives to natural selection had currency during this time, and McCosh stood firmly on the grounds of theistic evolution—the belief that evolution was completely in the hands of God.

It was during this same time that scientists also became more comfortable delving into matters that were once the domain of religion alone. Questions about race, class, and imperialism, for example, were steadily drifting into the realm of science, and there was a growing tendency among scientists to blur the lines between science and religion. A religious man himself, Osborn had some doubts about Darwin's theory, too. Disliking the randomness of natural selection, he thought it was too godless a process, and he was inclined to rationalize evolution as being more purpose driven.

Following the Western expedition, Osborn took a year off to study his fossils. At the same time, McCosh convinced him to pursue an advanced degree so that he might one day join the faculty of Princeton. Realizing, however, that there were hardly any appropriate graduate schools in America, Osborn decided to go abroad, moving to Cambridge, England, to study under the famous British anatomist Henry Balfour, and also Thomas Huxley, the well-known champion of Darwin.

While in England, Osborn briefly met the aged Charles Darwin. Osborn was working in Huxley's lab at the time, dissecting the nervous system of a lobster, as he described it in his journal—"I was leaning over my lobster (*Homarus vulgaris*) this morning, cutting away at the brain, I raised my head and looked up to see Huxley and Darwin passing by me . . . I went on apparently with skill, really hacking my brain away, and cast an occasional glance at the great old gray-haired man. I was startled, so unexpected was it, by Huxley speaking to me and introducing me to Darwin as 'An American who has already done some good paleontological work on the other side of the water.'" Osborn then described how he gave Darwin's hand "a tremendous squeeze."

Osborn's father was hardly pleased with his son's academic bent, but not because he was against having a scientist in the family. He had encouraged Henry's older brother Frederick in that direction, and had even arranged for him to meet with some of the scientists at the American Museum as a way of introducing him to the profession. Frederick had always been interested in natural history, and often met with his friend "Teddy" to exchange bird specimens. The Osborn family patriarch saw Frederick as the intellectual in the family, leaving Henry in line to carry on the family railroad business. This plan became even more hard-set when "Freddie" drowned in the Hudson River at the age of sixteen, having been pulled under by a strong current while swimming. It was the second untimely death for the Osborn family that summer, Henry's sister Virginia having died from illness not two months before.

After graduation, Henry was compelled to work in his father's railroad business. He could not avoid this fate, and had to at least give the life of a businessman a try. The elder Osborn had recently acquired the Chicago, Nashville, and New Orleans Railroads, and he wanted his son to help him run them. But Henry hated bookkeeping, and whether intentional or for lack of interest, he often lost track of bills. All he could think about was science, his mind perpetually drifting back to his fossils. He was a terrible businessman, and when his father finally realized this, he relented. He would permit his son to become a scientist so long as he pursued it with all his heart. He even built him a private library in the hope that he might one day master the pursuit of knowledge. Years later, the elder Osborn would quip that while his son was not a businessman, he could easily "write a book you cannot read!"

Having secured his doctoral degree, and successfully extricated himself from the family business in 1881, Osborn accepted a position as assistant professor of natural sciences at Princeton. That same year he married Lucretia Thatcher Perry, a dark-haired, elegant beauty and a descendant of Commodore Matthew Perry, the man who had opened Japan to the United States in the 1840s. "Loulu" also happened to be an acquaintance of Osborn's mother, Virginia, who was surprised to learn of her engagement to her son. Henry and Loulu had known each other for years, but neither family had any idea of their growing intimacy. Nonetheless, it was welcome news to Virginia because the two women were very much alike, both wishing to "live the same life—a life with Christ in God."

Their wedding was held at the Protestant Episcopal Church on Governor's Island, New York, where Lucretia's father was stationed as a general in the army, and they afterward returned to a beautiful garden party at Castle Rock. While they waited for their home to be built at Princeton, Henry and Loulu occupied a little house on William Street within walking distance of the campus. They called their humble residence "la Casita," and it was soon lampooned by a friend as "la Casita, in the Backstreeta."

As the newlyweds settled, Osborn fostered big dreams of distinguishing himself as a scholar at Princeton. For his research, he focused on comparative anatomy, using the subtle differences between different kinds of fossils as a means to reconstructing evolutionary history. Studying fossils in this way, he hoped to answer large-scale questions about how evolution worked.

The very idea that species evolved was an old one that went all the way back to the ancient Greeks. Osborn knew this deep history, but of all the pre-Darwinian thinkers, he was most influenced by the French botanist Jean-Baptiste Lamarck. As early as 1799, Lamarck had argued that the simplest organisms arose spontaneously, and that they became more intricate and specialized with time. Lamarck published his ideas in *Philosophie Zoologique* (1809), in which he proposed two laws. The first law stated that use or disuse of a body structure would cause it to grow or shrink over generations. Traits could be acquired as the organism adapted to environmental pressures. The second law asserted that such changes could be passed down to the organism's offspring, eventually creating new species. Together these laws suggested that species changed in a very direct way as they adapted to their environment.

To Lamarck, the history of living things was vertical and progressive—an upward series of transitions from single-celled organisms to increasingly complex creatures. Lamarck's most famous example of these laws was the neck of the giraffe. Because adult giraffes stretched their necks to browse on the highest leaves of a tree, he argued, their offspring were born with longer necks. Lamarck believed that humans arrived at their modern form by a similar process. For many, Lamarck's laws of acquired characteristics offered the simplest explanation for the transmutation of species, and at least at first, Osborn was among those believing in Lamarckism, if only because it allowed for direction and purpose in evolution.

Darwin threw a monkey wrench into Lamarck's way of thinking by introducing the concept of variation. With his publication of *On the Origin of Species* in 1859, Darwin presented an alternative to Lamarck's theory of use and disuse by proposing the selection of favored characteristics as the driver of evolution. According to Darwin, the evolutionary process was completely devoid of direction or purpose. Organisms evolved in response to any number of pressures coming from the environment, with those individuals having more advantageous traits tending to survive and reproduce. Direction, purpose, meaning, and progress had no part in the process. Evolution was blind, mechanical, and ultimately purposeless. As a process, Darwinian evolution was bleak and stark beyond what anyone at that time was prepared to imagine, and Osborn had a hard time accepting it.

But Osborn was right in sensing that there was something missing from both Darwin's and Lamarck's theories. Nothing was known of the factors by which traits were inherited. It was only after the discovery of Gregor Mendel's research on genetics in 1900, some thirty-five years after he first formulated the basic rules of heredity in 1865, that each of these theories was reconsidered in terms of genetic variation. Neo-Darwinism and Neo-Lamarckism were the terms used to describe these revised theories, as scientists continued to work toward settling on a unified theory of evolution. All this fascinated Osborn, and as a new Princeton professor, he was beginning to consider questions pertaining to the process of evolution as the core of his scientific research.

From the fossil record, Osborn saw evolution as a series of jumps. New characteristics arose, yet he was unable to find any evidence of intermediate forms showing the partial development of these features. Fossils seemed to suddenly appear in the geological record with new anatomical features fully formed. This swayed Osborn toward adopting an essentially Neo-Lamarckian explanation of evolution. At least in the early years of Osborn's career, Neo-Lamarckism seemed to be a better explanation of evolution than anything Darwin's theory had to offer.

Osborn modified his Neo-Lamarckian tendencies only after studying the work of the cytologist August Weismann, who proposed his "germ theory" of heredity. Weismann argued that only changes to the cells of the reproductive system of an organism—the germ plasm—could be passed on to offspring, and that changes to the nonreproductive body cells could not. It all made perfect sense because sperm and egg were the means by which genes were passed on. Only changes to these cells could be transmitted to the next generation. Darwinists argued that it was such changes in the gametes that constitute the raw material upon which natural selection worked, along with other pressures such as natural variation and the environment. This Neo-Darwinian concept seemed to be more tenable to Osborn, and it shifted his thinking so that it was somewhere between both Lamarck and Darwin; he incorporated elements of both in his way of thinking about evolution. Yet, no matter how logical the Neo-Darwinian way of thinking was, Osborn could never quite let go of God, and he forever held on to the notion of design and purpose in his evolutionary thinking.

As far as Osborn was concerned, there were still many unanswered questions as to how evolution really worked, and he was eager to uncover some groundbreaking law all his own. He could never bring himself to accept an interpretation of the history of life that was based on the inheritance of chance variations. And regardless of whether it was Neo-Darwinism, or Neo-Lamarckism, or something in between, Osborn was concerned about how these evolutionary theories might impact the conduct of life. Heavily influenced by his religious upbringing, he felt that in addition to fitting the facts, a good theory of evolution had to reinforce social order, too. He could never bring himself to accept an interpretation of evolution that had undesirable social consequences.

Although he loved Princeton, which in the late nineteenth century was a rather sleepy college, Osborn realized he could never hope to make an impact in his field while still based there. He needed to be in a museum where he could have access to all kinds of fossils. He had been offered a position as paleontologist at the American Museum early in his career, but turned it down because he did not wish to enter into the ongoing bone war between Marsh and Cope. But with their domination of the field cooling off a bit, he started to reconsider.

Still very much under the influence of his religious upbringing, Osborn certainly wanted to make a name for himself in science, but he also wanted to contribute something meaningful to society, and he saw the American Museum as the best place to do both. As he explained it to his father, the museum would enable him to have assistants, and with ample access to new fossils, he was fairly confident that he would be able to "discover some new laws" governing evolution.

Equally important to Osborn was his sense that the museum's leaders shared his values. The museum's president, Morris Jessup, was a deeply religious man, and committed to using the museum to convey moral lessons. Osborn's own background, a mashup of science and religion, dovetailed well with Jessup's instincts. The trustees, too, wanted the AMNH to teach both scientific and moral lessons, and they often discussed "the higher ideals which contemplation of nature was thought to encourage." The mandate for the men leading the American Museum was as much about social indoctrination as it was about scientific investigation, and this mattered to Osborn.

By the time Osborn arrived at the AMNH, he was convinced that nature was "the visible expression of the divine order of things" and that evolution was merely the process that "begins and ends the purposes of god." Thus he was resolved to promote not only his science but also his moral and social values, too. Exactly how he would go about doing so was only beginning to take shape in his mind, but of one thing Henry Fairfield Osborn was certain—the museum had the power to get his message across.

CHAPTER THREE

Shouldn't He Be Put Away?

Theodore Roosevelt narrowed his eyes. He was no art critic, but he knew good taxidermy when he saw it, and the deer head on the wall before him was exquisite. It was not just the size of the stag's antlers that impressed him but rather how the taxidermist had captured the spirit of an animal looking for a fight. With flared nostrils and wild eyes, *The Challenge* depicted a rutting buck in the moment of its call to combat. The governor of New York state, Roosevelt had been asked to judge the taxidermy competition at the 1895 Sportsman's Show, which was held in New York City, on account of his reputation as a naturalist. Always a keen observer of wildlife, and the author of several books on western hunting, he was America's foremost expert on big game.

Certainly weighing on Roosevelt's mind as he judged each animal was the fact that the white-tailed deer was almost entirely extirpated from his home state. They survived in appreciable numbers only in the Adirondacks. Deer were rare, but with their decline also came an end to the manly tradition of hunting—both matters of grave concern to Roosevelt. More than just an exquisite work of taxidermy, the deer head on the wall was a vivid reminder of all that could be lost, and an urgent call to save the American national character as expressed through hunting. Taking one last look at all the taxidermy around him, Roosevelt's choice for the winner was clear–*The Challenge* deserved first prize. But where was the taxidermist? Roosevelt wanted to meet Carl Akeley and shake his hand, but the man was gone, and it would be years before their lives intersected again.

Akeley had been practicing the art of taxidermy ever since he was a boy. A brooding introvert by nature, he liked nothing more than to wander the woods and fields of his family's farm alone. He preferred the solitude of nature to chattering people, and the gray winter days of western New York state were a comfort to him. A lackluster student, he seemed destined to a life of farming–to standing behind the plow and churning the gummy clay soil. Then one day in 1876, when he was just twelve years old, Carl Akeley discovered the art of taxidermy, and his life was changed forever.

Sent running to a neighbor's house for a basket of eggs, Akeley found the woman crying over her pet canary. She had accidently left its cage uncovered and the bird died in the chill of the night. Carl had seen the canary alive many times before, and he tried to console the woman: "I can fix the canary for you," he said. "It won't sing, but I think I can make it look as if it could." He wrapped the bird in a red bandanna and carried it home to his room. There he carefully skinned the bird and stuffed it, adding two small beads from his mother's sewing kit for eyes. Positioning the canary on a cut branch, and with its head slightly tilted in an attitude of listening, the bird looked as if it were alive. When Carl saw how much his handiwork soothed the distraught woman's feelings, he knew he had found his calling.

Determined to learn more about the mysterious art of taxidermy, Carl noticed a popular how-to book advertised in the January 6, 1876, edition of *The Youth's Companion*. Sylvester's *Taxidermist's Manual* promised to give "full instructions in Skinning, Mounting and Preserving Birds, Animals, Reptiles, Fishes, Skeletons, Insects, Eggs &c." Unfortunately, the book's 1 dollar price was more than he could bragged that his notes and photographs contained "more information on whales, living and dead, than had been gathered since whale hunting first began," and he was probably right.

All his travels around Japan solidified Andrews's fascination with the Far East. A typical Westerner, he had fallen for the so-called Asian mystique—the romanticized notion of the Orient as a land of mystical sensuality—and after living in Japan for nearly eight months, he had developed a profound affinity for the country. Years later, Andrews acknowledged that his decision to stay in Japan in 1910 "probably changed the whole course of my life."

When he was not working at a whaling station, Andrews immersed himself in Japanese culture. He studied local customs and ate nothing but native food. He frequented the markets and craft shops. He visited teahouses and watched geishas perform. He attended Kabuki theaters and explored the countryside. Armed with passable Japanese, he was determined to sample every aspect of Japanese life, even going so far as to spend an evening in a foul-smelling opium den where his first experience with the drug left him violently ill. As he would later confess, he was "extremely susceptible to cocaine, heroin, morphine, and hashish." He readily admitted that he had "tried them all to satisfy my insatiable curiosity," but he was quick to add that he also "learned to avoid them all like the plague."

Andrews developed a genuine liking for the Japanese, and wrote of feeling "completely at home" among them, even overcoming some of the customs that he at first found disconcerting, such as the exposed unisex toilets and the public baths that opened directly onto the street. There was not only a complete lack of privacy, but as a foreigner, he was the subject of endless curiosity. At Shimizu, crowds of people punched holes through the rice paper walls of his hotel room to stare at him day and night.

While at Aikawa, Andrews occupied a picturesque cottage overlooking the bay. It was located in the station master's compound, and it came with a "servant girl" named Kinu, whom Andrews described as "tiny, pretty, delicate and eighteen years old." She cooked his meals, kept the house clean, and ironed his clothes. She took care of Andrews for two weeks while he was struck down with a mysterious fever, never leaving him except to make visits to the local temple to pray for his swift recovery. Andrews regarded her with affection, calling her "a beautiful butterfly fluttering about in a flowered kimono . . . the huge bow of her obi always neatly arranged." He surprised her with gifts, and took her shopping for kimonos.

Finally, when the whaling season at Aikawa ended in late August, Andrews shipped several dozen crates of whale bones back to New York, visited Mother Jesus one last time, and faced the fact that it was time to go home. He was extraordinarily happy in Japan, and lingered just a few more weeks before finally taking the long way back to America, traveling there via Ceylon, Egypt, and Europe.

Arriving in New York in January 1911, Andrews was already planning his next Asian adventure, but the AMNH had changed in the seventeen months he was away. The museum's longtime president, Morris Jessup, had died in 1908, and then shortly afterward the director, Herman Bumpus, resigned and was replaced by Frederick A. Lucas, a naturalist and authority on Atlantic whales. Lucas had spent more than two decades at the Smithsonian Institution before moving to the AMNH, but the changes at the museum were such that it was now Henry Fairfield Osborn, the president of the board of trustees, who wielded all the power. Soon afterward, Osborn resigned his professorship at Columbia so that he could focus entirely on the museum.

Osborn would prove to be crucial to the development of Andrews's career. And whereas Bumpus was always tasking Andrews with errands, Osborn was more attuned to his sense of adventure. Drawn to what he called the romance of natural history, Osborn was more of a showman, always seeking to create an aura of intrigue about the museum.

Osborn and Andrews seemed made for each other. Seeking fame

and excitement, Andrews always had to justify his expeditions with scientific purpose, but Osborn was just the opposite. He was driven by scientific questions first, but at the same time he had an almost Barnumesque flair for showmanship. The two formed a kind of symbiotic relationship that fueled both of their careers, and while Andrews was really expert at stroking his new mentor's ego to his benefit, Osborn took full advantage of Andrews's charm and charisma to push his agendas.

Soon after returning from his around-the-world sojourn, Andrews sat down with Osborn for a business lunch. His purpose was to lay out an ambitious plan for a return trip to East Asia. While living in Japan the previous year, he had learned about a whale called *koku kujira*. They were reported along the coast of Korea, where they appeared in the fall and spring on their annual migration to and from the Arctic. Andrews never actually saw this particular kind of whale, which was called the devil fish, but he suspected that they might be a species that zoologists thought was extinct—the California gray whale.

Gray whales had once frequented the Pacific coasts of North America during their annual migrations, but intensive hunting had long since extirpated them. Andrews was intent on visiting Korea to find out if the devil fish was the same kind of whale that was once common off the coast of California. But whales were not Andrews's only objective, and he hoped to use the trip to make a transition to exploring East Asia on land.

Meeting with Osborn, Andrews proposed to study and explore the approach to Paik-tu-san, or Long White Mountain—a nine-thousand-foot volcanic peak on the Korea-Manchuria border. It acquired its name from the thick layer of white pumice covering its summit. A British explorer and mystic named Francis Younghusband had summited the mountain in 1879, and from the top he described vast forests stretching to the south. Writing in his 1896 book describing his explorations—*The Heart of a Continent*—Younghusband recounted in dramatic prose how the region had never really been explored, and how nobody knew "what secrets it concealed." It was too much for Andrews, who immediately decided that he would be the one to reveal its secrets. He wrote to Younghusband seeking advice, and the explorer responded advising him to go in from the Korean side and make a traverse of the forest to the base of the mountain. Andrews was sure he could make a significant contribution to geographical exploration, and along the way he planned to collect some rare and exotic specimens for the museum.

While Osborn saw the merits of investigating the devil fish, he was not impressed with the idea of exploring the mountains. He did not say no, but rather told Andrews that if he could raise the money himself, he could go ahead and do it as something of a side trip. Meanwhile, Andrews continued his studies at Columbia, hoping to finish up his doctoral degree in zoology. At the same time, he kept up his public speaking engagements, and continued writing articles on whales and Japan. It took Andrews less than a year to raise the money he needed for his expedition, after which the museum promoted him to assistant curator of mammals.

In December 1911, Andrews departed from San Francisco on the *Shinyo Maru* for Japan, reaching his beloved Yokohama in time to attend a New Year's Eve party given by Mother Jesus at Number Nine. Soon afterward, he traveled to a station owned by the Oriental Whaling Company at Ulsan, on Korea's eastern coast. It was a "very merry place," he reported, meaning that they did a lot of heavy drinking while they worked. Because he had arrived at the peak of the whaling season, he had no trouble proving what he had suspected—that the mysterious devil fish was indeed the gray whale.

Andrews had solved the problem of the whale's apparent extinction by proving that it was still thriving on the other side of the ocean. Prior to his investigations, naturalists were simply unaware that this species, which normally resided in the Arctic, had two migration routes, one down each side of the Pacific. Andrews examined and collected data on more than forty gray whales taken at that station, and then went to sea to observe and record their habits. He also acquired two complete skeletons for the museum's collections before turning his attention to his planned exploration of the Long White Mountain.

At this time, Korea was a territory of Japan under the rule of a military government. Aided by the US consul in Seoul and the Korean Bureau of Foreign Affairs, Andrews secured travel permits and letters of introduction to the Japanese commanders of a series of military outposts along the way to the mountain. He was joined by a Japanese interpreter who spoke Korean and a little bit of English, and also a Korean cook named Kim.

Early in April 1912, Andrews, Kim, and the interpreter left Seoul by train laden with camping gear, scientific equipment, and provisions. They boarded a ship at Pusan on the east coast, and sailed north to Seshin, from where they traveled overland to Musan, the largest city in northeastern Korea. Here Andrews was waylaid for weeks hunting a mysterious tiger that had reportedly killed six children and untold numbers of pigs, chickens, and dogs. As Andrews later described it, he was implored by the terrified villagers to shoot this tiger, and they practically begged him not to move on until he had done so. He spent three weeks there before finally giving up, never having seen the mysterious "Great Invisible," as the creature was known.

Finally, with pack horses and drivers secured at Musan, the expedition set out on its original objective. As they approached the mountain, the vegetation became thick and overgrown with oak and birch trees, and their progress was severely hampered by marshes and moss-covered logs. With each mile the forest grew thicker. At times, Andrews recalled that "the forest became so thick we had to cut our way through the tangled branches." It was difficult to proceed, and the entire party was growing despondent. As they climbed higher toward the foothills of the mountain, the oak and birch gave way to tall larches that allowed very little light to filter down to the ground. Although Andrews had never expected to find the region teeming with mammals, he was disappointed to find the place so deathly still.

Unrelenting rain made everything worse, and for a time his party threatened to leave him behind. One of their biggest fears was that they would become hopelessly lost. "The silence . . . of the forest began to work upon the imagination of the Koreans," Andrews wrote, "and after we had been threading our way for five days through the mazes of an untouched wilderness the natives were discouraged and asked to return." But just then, they caught a glimpse of the majestic Long White Mountain rising out of the forest, and "banked to the top with snow," Andrews observed. "It looked like a great white cloud that had settled to earth for a moment's rest. The open sky and the mountain acted like magic on my men. They began to talk and sing and call to each other in laughing voices. That night we camped in the shadow of the mountain."

Andrews slept for fifteen hours, utterly exhausted. They had crossed the impenetrable forests that Younghusband had described earlier and reached the base of the mountain. He would make no attempt to climb it—that was not his mission—but rather he spent weeks collecting zoological specimens at the base. From there he went south and west to the Yalu River, exploring and collecting as he went. In the end, it took him five months to complete the 375-mile trip through the wilderness.

Throughout the overland expedition, Andrews had not seen another White traveler and had spoken only Japanese. He had not received any news from the outside world until he met an American missionary—a Dr. Gale—on the train to Seoul. Gale was horrified when Andrews told him of his plans to make his way back to the United States by going overland across Asia, and then after visiting Europe, to cross the Atlantic on a new ship called the *Titanic.* He had no idea that the ship had sunk on its maiden voyage.

By the time he reached his hotel in Seoul, Andrews was six weeks overdue, and reports had already circulated of the expedition's presumed demise in the wilds of the Manchurian frontier. Several newspapers had repeated the story, and he arrived to find a number of frantic messages. He had to quickly reassure everyone that he was still very much alive. Unfortunately, simply surviving was hardly sufficient, and the arduous exploration had yielded little in the way of scientific discoveries. He had collected just 162 mammals, which was not much, considering they were mostly chipmunks, hamsters, and mice. Despite what seemed to be disappointing results, however, the expedition had the one redeeming quality of establishing his credentials as a land explorer, which was all he ever wanted in the first place.

PART II

LIFE MISSIONS

CHAPTER EIGHT

The Romance of Natural History

Carl Akeley and Roy Chapman Andrews exemplified a kind of taut masculinity that many Americans believed was under threat around the turn of the twentieth century. It was all thought to be the result of the nation's transformation into an urban and industrial society, which forced men out of traditional farming and ranching occupations, and into more sedentary desk jobs. Men were losing something vital, it was believed, and becoming overly feminized. The physician George M. Beard had coined the term *neurasthenia* for this loss of vitality, and in 1869 he described how it left men aimless, indecisive, and fearful. Beard characterized the disease as afflicting intellectuals especially, and he claimed it was the result of too much civilization. So great was this fear that by the end of the nineteenth century the condition was being referred to as *overcivilization*, and it was thought to be putting masculinity at risk.

Theodore Roosevelt was especially vocal about this erosion of manhood. Advocating what he called *the strenuous life*, he touted physical exertion and rugged individualism as a remedy. Speaking on the subject while on the campaign trail in Chicago in 1899, he rallied his audience to take action on behalf of the nation—"I wish to preach, not the doctrine of ignoble ease, but the doctrine of the strenuous life, the life of toil and effort, of labor and strife to preach that highest form of success which comes, not to the man who desires mere easy peace, but to the man who does not shrink from danger, from hardship, or from bitter toil, and who out of these wins the splendid ultimate triumph."

In particular, Roosevelt felt that men needed to experience conquests in the outdoors. "We are a nation of hunters and frequenters of the forest, plains, and waters," he declared. To Roosevelt, hunting was the ultimate training for manhood, and the sport was often prescribed as the cure for overcivilization. "Let us have more hunters and more hunting in America," said Fordham University medical professor James J. Walsh, "and we shall have far fewer nervous breakdowns."

At the AMNH, Henry Fairfield Osborn embraced Roosevelt's philosophy, and went a step further by intertwining the strenuous life with his own ideas about evolution. Osborn believed that twentieth-century men had so lost their drive that they were no longer part of the evolutionary struggle for existence. He feared American men had dead-ended, and that the national character was suffering. Heeding Roosevelt's call, Osborn built on the strong parallel between sport hunting and scientific collecting. If hunting was the cure for flagging American manhood, then museum collectors—whom many considered huntsmen par excellence because they hunted for science—were primed to play an especially meaningful role in reinvigorating manhood.

Camping out in the wilderness, and shooting and preserving wild birds and mammals for natural history museums, was a higher form of hunting because it had scientific research, and not mere sport, as its ultimate goal. More than just seeking a trophy, Akeley and Andrews hunted for specimens that might prove to be entirely new species, or that would lead to some new understanding of the way nature worked. They were not just hunting familiar animals but also seeking obscure and little-known species in some of the remotest parts of the world. Using both brains and brawn, museum men hunted for a higher intellectual purpose. What could be manlier than that?

Osborn wished to promote both Carl Akeley and Roy Chapman Andrews as role models of manliness. Both had just returned from their respective expeditions to Africa and Asia, and they embodied a certain muscular naturalism that made them the poster children of what Osborn liked to call "the romance of natural history." A romantic himself, Osborn saw the entire history of life on Earth as a series of epic battles for survival in which species evolved by tooth and claw. Osborn wished to capitalize on the fact that he had such swashbuckling men as Akeley and Andrews in his museum.

As president of the American Museum, Osborn moved to personify the excitement of exploration at the institution. Not only did this approach resonate well with Americans anxious about overcivilization, but it also promoted a more traditional kind of research that especially appealed to Osborn. Like Roosevelt, he disliked the growing popularity of laboratory science, with its bubbling beakers and controlled experiments, and he yearned for a return to the more traditional method of observing nature directly in the field. Seeking to romanticize field exploration, Osborn studiously avoided using the words "science" and "scientist," thinking them too effete. He preferred "natural history" and "naturalist" instead, believing they had a more romantic ring.

Osborn's emphasis on adventurous expeditions was in keeping with a tone that had been set by Morris Jessup in the early years of the museum. A strong supporter of exploration, Jessup had launched the museum's first expedition when he sent J. A. Allen out to Montana to collect bison in 1888. It was only shortly after this first expedition that Osborn hired a cadre of fossil hunters to make annual collecting trips to the western states and territories. He very skillfully dramatized these fossil digs as "expeditions into the past," and he sketched out plans to have any dinosaur skeletons they found articulated in the museum's exhibit halls. He wanted everyone to see these extinct creatures not just as so many boxes of bones but also as real animals in dramatic freestanding poses.

Osborn further evoked the romance of natural history by hiring a young artist named Charles R. Knight, whose melodramatic renderings of prehistoric life would fill the museum's exhibit halls. From Knight's imagination came works of stalwart mammoths marching across bleak Ice Age scenes, saber-toothed cats descending on camels mired in tar pits, as well as the dire drama of fur-clad men fending off a cave bear with sharpened sticks and stones. Dramatizing prehistoric life as a constant struggle, Knight brought these lost worlds to life in a way that especially appealed to Osborn.

The American Museum had always created exhibits with an eye toward city dwellers. Indeed, the institution was founded on the premise that city folk needed a connection to the restorative powers of nature. It was among the first museums to really embrace habitat groups as idyllic windows into nature, and from their first appearance in the late 1800s, these dioramas were designed to nurture a reverence of nature by creating the illusion of its beauty.

Every one of the museum's habitat dioramas—some of the earliest of which can still be seen in the museum's Hall of Ocean Life—provided museumgoers with the opportunity to have a transformational wilderness experience right in the heart of New York City. Walking from one habitat scene to another, visitors could take in vignettes of animals caring for their young, or fighting for the chance to breed. Visually arresting, these exhibits also reinforced social hierarchies, and promoted a more traditional lifestyle in harmony with nature. In this way, the habitat dioramas of the American Museum dosed New York's poorest urban dwellers—many of them immigrants—with a dram of carefully measured morality from nature.

While all this messaging about manliness and the virtues of nature had deep roots in the American Museum, it was dramatically amplified in response to the rapid societal changes taking place at the turn of the twentieth century. Immigration was one of the most contentious of issues. Hundreds of thousands of new immigrants were arriving on America's shores with each passing year, but unlike the German and Scandinavian immigrants of previous years, who came to settle new farms on the frontier, the newest waves of huddled masses were more likely to come from southern and eastern Europe. Many of these new immigrants were also Jews, and they were prone to settling in the city, in the hopes of filling demand for urban labor. New York was so overwhelmed with immigrants looking for a better life that they surpassed the city's ability to accommodate them. Slums were the result, and in them many saw a cacophony of foreign languages, strange customs, filth, rising chaos, and crime.

To the wealthy patricians in charge at the American Museum—men who for so long enjoyed social deference and privilege—these new immigrants were an existential threat. Populating Manhattan's Lower East Side, they cared little for the prestigious families of old New York, and their apparent lack of a connection to nature was thought to signify an inferior moral character. To New York's old moneyed elites, it was no wonder that these Lower East Siders were so beholden to corrupt Tammany Hall—the Democratic political machine that provided them with food, shelter, and jobs in exchange for their votes.

Osborn and the museum's trustees hoped to counter these new immigrants by projecting a more traditional way of life, and habitat dioramas were a big part of their answer. "If these people cannot go to the country, then the Museum must bring nature to the city," Osborn said. It was as if, by showcasing idyllic families of endangered animals on the vanishing frontier, they might set a tone for saving themselves and their own way of life in their besieged city.

Such was the tone for the AMNH at the outset of the twentieth century. Nature was the bulwark by which the older and more established White Protestants of old New York hoped to push back against the changing tide of social mores. Nature—and more specifically, man's conquering of nature by way of the hunt—became paramount. Although never a hunter himself, Osborn joined ranks with a small but influential circle of men focused on the plight of North America's big-game mammals. Theodore Roosevelt was the most famous and outspoken of this bunch, and together with George Bird Grinnell, he founded the Boone and Crockett Club to promote the virtues of hunting. But more than anyone else, Osborn was influenced by someone less-well-known today—Madison Grant.

Henry Fairfield Osborn and Madison Grant seemed destined to become lifelong friends. Both hailed from wealthy New York City families, and although neither had to work for a living, they were nonetheless ambitious in the extreme. An avid big-game hunter, Grant joined the founders of the Boone and Crockett Club in putting that organization at the vanguard of America's nascent wildlife conservation movement. He helped to create Glacier and Denali National Parks, and cofounded the Redwoods League and the Bison Society to save these two majestic species from annihilation. Although it may seem ironic for a hunter to play such an important role in protecting species, Grant was as much interested in saving the *pastime* of hunting as he was in the animals themselves.

As Grant hunted the dwindling big-game mammals of North America, he dreamed of creating a zoological park where the last survivors of any endangered species could live. Firmly believing that the elk, pronghorn, mountain sheep, and bison were doomed to extirpation in the wild, he sought to create a last refuge for these animals in surroundings that closely matched their native habitat. "No civilized nation," he stated, "should allow its wild animals to be exterminated without at least making an attempt to preserve living representatives of all species that can be kept alive in confinement."

Grant sought to locate his zoo in the middle of New York City, but he didn't want to create a typical nineteenth-century menagerie. New York already had the Central Park Zoo, which was crammed full of flea-bitten camels, bears, and monkeys. "A more wretched exhibition of ill-kept specimens," Grant exclaimed, "cannot be found in any large city in the world." He was disgusted with the idea of confining animals in solitary cells behind thick iron bars, and he was determined to make his zoological park something else. He envisioned a zoo occupying hundreds of acres, so that the animals could live together in groups exactly as they would have in the wild. To the greatest extent possible, he wanted to feature these endangered animals as they existed in nature.

Some experts thought Grant's idea was too extreme, and that his zoo wouldn't be very popular. They argued that the public actually liked seeing solitary animals in small cages, if only to get a better look at them. Fortunately, there were plenty of others who thought otherwise, and they were intrigued by Grant's idea of an urban zoological park. At the time, the American character was widely believed to have been forged on the frontier, thanks to the teachings of the historian Frederick Jackson Turner, and there was a growing movement to put new immigrants in touch with the natural setting in which America's values had first flourished. Museum dioramas were one way of doing this, but so, too, were zoos. Madison Grant's idea seemed like a very American thing to support.

Dreams of zoological gardens were one thing, but as a die-hard Republican, Grant had to battle the city's infamously corrupt Tammany Hall politicians, who had essentially bought the votes of nearly every new immigrant. As Grant's friend Rudyard Kipling once quipped, New York City was "a despotism of the alien, by the alien, for the alien, tempered with occasional insurrections of decent folk." As it turned out, the year 1894 saw one of those brief insurrections in the form of Grant leading a band of civic reformers to expose Tammany Hall. It was no easy task because New York City had over 1.8 million residents, of whom an astounding 1.4 million were new immigrants. Foreigners outnumbered old-stock Americans three to one, leading one of Grant's associates to declare that "New York is now a great foreign city with an American quarter." Grant was personally distressed by the influx of so many foreigners, which to him seemed more like an invasion. In the crowded slums of the Lower East Side, crime and drunkenness were rife, making that part of the city all but unlivable.

Remarkably, Grant got his opposition candidate elected and sworn in as mayor of New York City, and although William Strong only survived for one term, it opened a window of opportunity. As Grant's friend Theodore Roosevelt put it, if he was ever going to turn his dream for a zoo into a reality, now was the moment. Grant quickly drafted a bill for the creation of the New York Zoological Society, a corporation empowered to establish a zoological park somewhere in New York City. The bill passed and was signed into law in April 1895. "I congratulate you with all my heart upon your success with the Zoo bill," Roosevelt wrote Grant. As a former New York state assemblyman, he spoke from experience—"Really, you have done more than I hoped. I always count myself lucky if I get one out of three or four measures through."

Having successfully brought the New York Zoological Society into existence, Grant refrained from serving as its first president. That title went to Levi Morton, the former vice president of the United States under Benjamin Harrison. Instead, Grant agreed to share the lesser role of secretary with George Bird Grinnell. Yet everyone knew that Grant was the force behind the society and the future zoo, and he kept control by stocking the executive board with friends from within his social circle. Paramount among Grant's crony appointments was Henry Fairfield Osborn, who would eventually supplant Levi Morton as president of the Zoological Society, just as Madison Grant would eventually play an outsized role on the board of the AMNH. Grant and Osborn would work together for decades to shape both the Bronx Zoo and the American Museum of Natural History to fit their own social beliefs.

To actually run the day-to-day business of the zoo, Grant and Osborn appointed William Temple Hornaday as director. The innovative taxidermist, who had started out at Ward's and later became the chief taxidermist at the Smithsonian's United States National Museum, may not have seemed the most logical choice to run a collection of living animals. However, Hornaday's interest in taxidermy was very much rooted in his desire to save endangered species. It was while he was working as a taxidermist for the Smithsonian that Hornaday had gone on an expedition to Montana to collect specimens of bison, and he was stunned to find the species very nearly extinct. This was the beginning of his lifelong commitment to wildlife conservation, and it drove him to create the Smithsonian's National Zoo in 1889. A full six years before Grant even entertained the notion of establishing the Bronx Zoo, Hornaday had created and run the largest and most important zoo in America—and all from the tiny seed of taxidermy. He was definitely the best choice for running the Bronx Zoo. A onetime avid big-game hunter, Hornaday abandoned the sport in order to devote himself to the protection of wildlife, and he made the move from the Smithsonian's National Zoo to New York's Bronx Zoo in 1896 to further this cause.

Hornaday's first task as director was to select a site for the new zoo. He needed to find a plot of land that was big enough to accommodate the needs of a large and diverse collection of species, yet still be accessible to the public. Surveying all the undeveloped plots of land in the city, Hornaday eventually settled on Bronx Park. As he remembered it, Bronx Park "was an unbroken wilderness, to the eye almost as wild and unkempt as the heart of the Adirondacks." When he first saw the site, he had the feeling of "almost paralyzing astonishment and profound gratitude. It seemed incredible that such virgin forest . . . had been spared in the City of New York until 1896!" Negotiations ensued, and Grant convinced the city to deed the Zoological Society all of Bronx Park south of Pelham Avenue, a tract of land totaling some 261 acres.

Grant and Osborn raised funds for the zoo, and as construction began, they joined Hornaday in helping to design uniforms, hire staff, and procure animals. Although well respected for his expertise, Hornaday nonetheless experienced glitches. Some of the first few animals added to the new zoo promptly escaped, like the group of sea lions that fled to the Bronx River. And when an aggressive sixteen-foot python slithered out through a hole in its enclosure, the short-tempered Hornaday blurted out, "Is this the way to start a new Zoological Park?" He even took some animals home, such as when a group of orangutans arrived before their pen was complete. Hornaday's wife, Josephine, took care of them in their living room.

Despite all these setbacks, the zoo began to take shape, housing some 843 animals representing 157 different species. Finally, on November 8, 1899, the Bronx Zoo opened to the public. Speaking at its inauguration, Osborn praised the new zoo: "All the animals of North America . . . will be seen just as they live in the woods—happier perhaps because safe from the rifle of the hunter, free from the keen struggle for existence, generously quartered and fed." He stressed the educational purpose of the zoo, noting that it would bring the "wonders and beauties" of nature within the reach of the thousands and millions of all classes who cannot travel or explore.

Grant, Osborn, and Hornaday would go on to run the zoo through its first three decades of existence. For all three men, nature preservation was part of a larger concern for preserving traditional ideals and values about race, class, and society. Yet even as they touted their best intentions, they could not help but be frustrated with the very people they supposedly wanted to help. Especially after the subway line was extended to the Bronx, and the denizens of the Lower East Side visited in greater numbers, they found it hard to contain their contempt for the "degenerates" who babbled in foreign languages, dozed on the lawns, and trashed the grounds of the park. Hornaday went so far as to sniff that most of the zoo's visitors were "low-lived beasts who appreciate nothing, and love filth and disorder."

Nostalgia for a bygone way of American life was one thing, but the zoo took a turn toward the extreme when it put a living African pygmy on display in the Primate House in 1906. It all began when a quasi-missionary-explorer named Samuel Phillips Verner went to Africa to bring back some pygmies for an "ethnographic exhibit" at the St. Louis World's Fair. Verner had been hired by Dr. William McGee, who was hoping to legitimize the new science of anthropology with a sprawling exhibit he called *The University of Man*, in which he displayed "representatives of all the world's races, ranging from the smallest pygmies to the most gigantic peoples, from the darkest blacks to the dominant whites."

Such exhibits were hardly scandalous at the time, and the American Museum had done something just as bad when, in 1897, the Arctic explorer Robert Peary returned from Greenland with six "Eskimos" for the museum. Within a matter of months, four of these individuals died of tuberculosis, after which the renowned anthropologist Franz Boas had their skeletons stripped of flesh and added to the museum's collection. There was hardly a shrug about this from the public, but several years later, the surviving son of one of the deceased—a boy named Minik—was horrified to find his father's skeleton on display in one of the museum's exhibit halls.

Verner went off into the interior of Africa to buy from slave traders—for the price of a pound of salt and a bolt of cloth—a twenty-one-year-old pygmy man named Ota Benga. Bringing him back to America, Verner delivered Ota Benga to Dr. McGee. The man would be exhibited at the St. Louis World's Fair, but with the promise from Verner that he would return him to his native Africa when all was done. Verner lived true to his promise, but once back in his homeland, Ota Benga no longer felt comfortable among his own people. Trying to settle down, he married a Batwa woman, but she died of snakebite. Eventually Ota Benga asked Verner to take him back to America.

Returning to New York in 1906, the virtually penniless Verner was not quite sure what to do with his African companion. For a short time, he stayed in a spare room at the American Museum while Verner tried to sell them a live chimpanzee that he had brought back from Africa. From there, Verner went up to the Bronx Zoo, where

Hornaday bought the chimp, and as part of the deal, agreed to let Ota Benga stay at the zoo. Hornaday's only stipulation was that all parties had to agree that Ota Benga still "belonged" to Verner, and that he would eventually have to take him back.

At first, Ota Benga spent his days at the Bronx Zoo walking around the grounds wearing normal western clothes. At the same time, Hornaday encouraged him to freely interact with some of the animals on exhibit, and he eventually grew very fond of an orangutan named Dohong. Described as the "presiding genius of the Monkey House," Dohong had been taught to wear pants and ride a tricycle, and she ate with a knife and fork. The zookeepers opened Dohong's cage whenever Ota Benga wished to visit her, and they encouraged him to set up his hammock in her enclosure.

This was the beginning of a slow but steady process of gradually transitioning Ota Benga from a man who spent his time wandering the zoo grounds to someone who ultimately ended up being displayed in a Monkey House cage. Seemingly amused with Ota Benga, Hornaday found it all too easy to bill him as one of the zoo's attractions. Finally, on Saturday September 8, 1906, the first headline appeared in *The New York Times*: "Bushman Shares a Cage with Bronx Park Apes." Throngs of curiosity seekers crowded the zoo, and Hornaday had a sign installed outside the enclosure at the Monkey House:

THE AFRICAN PYGMY, "OTA BENGA."

AGE, 23 YEARS. HEIGHT, 4 FEET 11 INCHES.
WEIGHT 103 POUNDS. BROUGHT FROM THE KASAI RIVER,
CONGO FREE STATE, SOUTH CENTRAL AFRICA,
BY DR. SAMUEL VERNER.

The improvised exhibit was extremely popular, as a front-page story in the *Times* attested: "There was always a crowd before the cage, most of the time howling with laughter." The children especially were reported to have "laughed uproariously," and one of the most amusing things, according to the *Times*, was that "the pygmy was not much taller than the orang-outang, and one had a good opportunity to study their points of resemblance. Their heads are much alike, and both grin in the same way when pleased." They were considered to be so similar that "many of those in the crowd who watched Benga's antics doubted if he was a human being."

Hornaday announced that "the little savage" would remain on display until late in the fall. When a reporter questioned the act of placing a man in a monkey cage, the director explained that "the little black man is really very comfortable there," adding glibly that he had "one of the best rooms in the primate house." It took the threat of a lawsuit from a committee of clergymen from the Colored Baptist Ministers' Conference to finally get Madison Grant to order that Ota Benga not be officially displayed at the zoo. Thus freed, Ota Benga still resided in the park—he had nowhere else to go—and he still returned to the Primate House to sleep every night.

Meanwhile, back at the AMNH, Osborn was busy studying the remains of extinct mammals. The museum held thousands of fossils documenting millions of years of evolutionary history. Spreading dozens of these fossils out on a tabletop in his office, he moved the old bones around like chess pieces while trying to infer the order in which they evolved. Not content with simply describing new species, Osborn sought to answer bigger questions about the very process of evolution. He disliked the randomness of natural selection and believed it did not adequately explain the mechanism of evolution. Osborn was still trying to work out a new evolutionary "law" all his own. Confident in his intellect, he felt that if he just examined enough fossils, it would only be a matter of time before he had some spark of inspiration.

Studying fossil horses in particular, Osborn noticed how their teeth evolved to become more specialized over time. He believed these changes arose in response to new challenges encountered during the animal's lifetime, and he was especially struck by how the teeth tended to evolve cusps at precisely the spots where, in older fossils, they had previously incurred the most wear. To Osborn, it appeared as if the teeth were responding to a specific need, and moreover, these same tooth cusps evolved in precisely the same way among species that were not even closely related.

Osborn interpreted these observations as proof that species evolved along set pathways, and that evolution was the expression of some latent, and almost *mystical* potential in an organism. The evolutionary process was not random, Osborn insisted, but rather emerged in response to the struggles a species endured as it invaded new and more challenging habitats. In a further twist, Osborn noted how certain animals that looked very similar could in fact be only distantly related, foreshadowing what would later be termed convergent evolution—a real evolutionary outcome that is widely accepted today.

Based on all the fossil evidence before him, and everything he knew about animal distributions, Osborn concluded that the vast majority of the living mammal groups must have had their origins in central Asia, and that they evolved into the various groups we see today as they radiated outward from this center. The known distributions of both living and fossil mammal species—many of which were known from Europe and western North America but not in-between—suggested central Asia as their logical point of origin.

Although derived from his studies of fossils, it was not long before Osborn applied this same thinking to the evolution of human races. For a long time, he had considered the evolution of human racial qualities, but never really followed through until after—as Grant's biographer Jonathan Spiro describes it—a fateful evening lecture he attended with his good friend Madison Grant.

The lecture took place on the night of February 6, 1908, and the venue was the Half Moon Club. Named after Henry Hudson's ship, the club was the creation of Grant and Osborn. By that time the two men had become so close that they communicated daily, either by telephone or letter, and dined together about once a week. Osborn also made a habit of visiting Grant at the Bronx Zoo most Saturdays, but on this particular night, they were both focused on the man who was about to give a lecture with a most interesting title—*The Migration of Races*.

William Z. Ripley was a Columbia University economist and the author of a great tome called *The Races of Europe* (1899). Ripley believed that race was crucial to understanding all of human history, but his real specialty was classifying European populations according to their anatomy. Drawing conclusions from the many ways in which human skulls vary in relation to their historical origin, Ripley believed he would uncover the most basic European racial "type" beneath the veneers of ethnicity and nationality. In this regard, Ripley was looking for the anatomical standard from which to compare all other racial types. To Ripley, race was something measured in the skull, and not to be confounded by culture, language, or national identity. "Race denotes what a man *is*; all these other details of social life represent what man *does*," Ripley explained. In other words, Ripley sought to analyze human populations as a mammalogist might classify different subspecies of mice.

According to Ripley, Europe was peopled not by one race but by three races. Northern Europe was home to the tall, long-headed "Teutons," or "Nordics" as Grant and Osborn preferred to call them, with their tendency toward light hair, blue eyes, and narrow noses. Central Europe had the stockier and round-headed "Alpines," with their more brownish hair, while in the south there were the long-headed "Mediterraneans," with their dark hair, dark eyes, and broad noses. These were just the most obvious external features that were most convenient for recognizing the three races, but Ripley backed up his claims with pages of additional measurements and qualitative descriptions.

All this was of immediate interest to Ripley's American audience because of the ever increasing "horde" of Alpines and Mediterraneans entering the United States each year. As Ripley liked to point out, such an influx of foreigners was causing "violent and volcanic dislocations" and threatening American society with disease, overcrowding, low wages, moral chaos, and political corruption. "The tide will rise higher," he predicted, until we are "inundated by the engulfing flood."

Ripley also expressed serious concerns about the effect of the newcomers on the nation's gene pool. "We have tapped the political sinks of Europe," lamented Ripley, the net result being the existence in America of "a congeries of human beings, unparalleled for ethnic diversity anywhere else on the face of the earth." All these fears revolved around one big question—what would happen if the Alpines and Mediterraneans began to intermarry with what they considered to be the dominant Nordic race already established in America? Osborn was sure he knew the answer. It would result in the dilution of America's superior genetic stock and the dissolution of the Nordics.

All this drivel in Ripley's lecture seems to have profoundly impacted both Grant and Osborn because it marked a distinct turning point in the courses of their research. Whereas Grant had up until this point concerned himself with the conservation of North American mammals—moose, elk, and bison—he was now more focused on what he believed to be the most endangered species of all—the Nordics. Likewise, Osborn had formulated his own ideas about evolution by looking at fossil mammals, only to become more focused on applying these ideas to human evolution. Whether these shifts were the result of the changing times, or the more direct influence of Ripley, is a matter of speculation, but the fact remains that Grant and Osborn changed the course of their research at this time.

Not long after Ripley's lecture, Morris K. Jessup died, and Osborn took his place as the president of the American Museum. Soon he would relinquish his professorship at Columbia in order to concentrate his efforts on making the American Museum his own. It was the beginning of the age of Grant and Osborn at the AMNH, and having begun their careers studying the evolution of mammals and the conservation of endangered species, the two resolved to write twin books on their new favorite subjects—the evolution of humans and the endangered White race. Striving together in lockstep, Osborn and Grant would advance their new agenda by focusing their research on the question of human evolution, with all its racial implications.

CHAPTER NINE

A Little Eye Gleaming Revenge

Carl Akeley found Theodore Roosevelt—somewhat dusty and sunburnt—on the plains of East Africa in 1909. His safari of more than two hundred men was easy enough to locate because they kicked up a cloud of dust that could be seen for miles. The last time the two men had spoken was during a White House dinner party about a year before. It was then that Akeley so regaled the president with stories of ferocious lions that Roosevelt—who had been planning to hunt bears in Alaska—changed his postpresidential plans and decided to go to Africa.

Roosevelt's safari was not his first trip to the Dark Continent. As a young boy, in 1872, Roosevelt had spent several weeks traveling though Egypt with his family. A budding naturalist, he had toted along his new shotgun so he could collect birds along the way. Although only fourteen years old, little Theodore had already amassed a sizable collection of natural history specimens in what he dubbed his "Roosevelt Museum" at home. Full of boyish enthusiasm, he regarded his museum seriously, took taxidermy lessons, and made sure that every one of his specimens was dutifully catalogued.

Roosevelt enrolled at Harvard with the intention of studying to become a naturalist. He aspired to be like one of the outdoor naturalists he had read about growing up—a man like John James Audubon, who sought to share the beauty of the birds he saw in the field, or Spencer Baird, the Smithsonian curator who had no qualms about amassing vast collections of zoological specimens.

Roosevelt wanted to study birds, and as a young man he was especially adept at identifying species by sound. He had already published some of his field observations by the time he was in college, and he kept meticulous records of the annual migrations of birds. The chance to combine vigorous outdoor activity with scholarly study appealed to him, but his hopes for becoming a field ornithologist were dashed when he realized that this kind of adventurous outdoor naturalism was going out of style. The so-called new biology was ascendant, having come across the Atlantic from Europe and taken hold in America. The new biology emphasized laboratory work and experimentation over field observation, but none of this appealed to Roosevelt. He didn't have the patience to sit at a microscope, and just wanted to get out into the woods with his gun. Much to his dismay, the kind of "naked eye science" that Roosevelt adored was already a thing of the past.

Abandoning his dream of becoming a professional ornithologist, Roosevelt went on to become a politician and statesman instead, but he never forgot his first love: nature. More critically, Roosevelt never lost sight of the importance of natural history collections. Throughout his life, Roosevelt donated specimens to both the AMNH and the Smithsonian Institution. He respected the work of museum naturalists, who despite the new biology still carried on the tradition of observing and collecting new specimens in the field. He kept an active correspondence with a number of museum curators, and eagerly followed their efforts to document the diversity of species from around the world. The turn of the twentieth century was a critical time for this kind of work, with the destruction of natural habitats threatening to erase entire chapters from the story of evolution.

As a young man, Roosevelt had seen how the advent of the transcontinental railroads led to the destruction of big game in the

American West, and he worried that the same thing was about to happen again in East Africa. The British had just completed the Uganda Railroad, and Roosevelt was sure it was only a matter of time before all of East Africa was transformed. This time, however, Roosevelt was in a greater position of power, and although he could not hold back the advance of civilization, he felt he could at least lead an effort to document the fauna of East Africa before its inevitable decline. Perhaps he could argue for the protection of certain unique areas, but in order to do so, he first needed to make a detailed study of how all the different kinds of animals were distributed across the land. Roosevelt recognized the importance of creating such a scientific record, and pledged to donate nearly all the large animals that he and his son Kermit would hunt to the Smithsonian's scientific research collections. What is more, he insisted that the Smithsonian bring along a team of trained naturalists to properly document the bird and small mammal fauna, too.

Roosevelt was sure he could do a lot of good by documenting the fauna of East Africa—one of the most spectacular faunal assemblages in the world. He understood the importance of collecting scientific specimens for posterity, and it was because of his deep understanding of museum work that he turned his hunting trip into a full-blown biological survey under the aegis of the Smithsonian Institution. Before he even packed up his rifles, Roosevelt's big-game hunt was transformed into a scientific expedition. It was the realization of Roosevelt's boyhood dream, and it was his way of thumbing his nose at the "new science" that he found so stifling in his younger years. He would now set things straight by showing that fieldwork was still relevant. Most parts of Africa, Asia, and South America were barely explored zoologically, and the scientists at the Smithsonian were eager to start surveying these unknown lands.

The secretary of the Smithsonian, Charles Wolcott, was quick to see the benefits of a partnership with Theodore Roosevelt, who was arguably the most famous man in the world. Natural history museums everywhere were struggling to voice their relevance to modern science. The joint scientific expedition would benefit both parties because Roosevelt could portray his African adventure as something more than a hunting trip, and the Smithsonian would gain exposure and notoriety from its association with the former president.

Roosevelt paid for his hunting with money secured from *Scribner's* to write a series of magazine articles, while the Smithsonian went to Andrew Carnegie for funds to support their scientists. Three experienced naturalists were recruited for the expedition: J. Edgar Mearns to collect birds, plants, and anthropological materials; Edmund Heller to preserve all the large mammals; and J. Alden Loring to round things out by trapping the smaller rats, mice, and shrews. Nothing like their expedition had ever been attempted before, and the Smithsonian stood to gain the most important collection of African specimens in the world.

The reunion of Carl Akeley and Theodore Roosevelt on the dusty plains of East Africa had been planned so that Akeley could forever link the famous president to his fieldwork and to the elephant exhibit at the American Museum. The Roosevelt name gave anything greater value, and their meeting was a very deliberate show of support for Akeley's work. All they needed to do now was get some elephants.

Carl and Delia had arrived in British East Africa by way of the port city of Mombasa a few months before, and just as they had done during their 1905 expedition, they boarded a special train of the Uganda Railway for Nairobi. But whereas in 1905 they had been encouraged by the wildlife they saw along the ride, this time around they were dismayed. In the years since their last visit, the landscape had changed. The vast panoramas were still there, dotted with occasional giraffe and zebra, but the great herds of game were all gone. Akeley was alarmed at the change, and although he was on a mission to preserve the memory of a doomed fauna, he faced the possibility that he might have arrived too late.

Nairobi, too, had changed since Akeley's last visit. It was no longer the hardscrabble outpost it had been before. Checking in with his former safari outfitting company, Newland, Tarlton & Co., he contracted 118 men for the expedition. Such a seemingly large number of men was required because everything had to be carried by a human porter, horses and mules being too susceptible to diseases transmitted by the tsetse fly. Food, tents, and the various and sundry cooking and camping supplies were essential just to survive, but added to these were the guns and ammunition needed to secure specimens. All kinds of knives, ropes, pulleys, and measuring devices were required to skin large mammals, but the most cumbersome and weighty supply of all was the large quantity of salt needed to cure the hides of the animals. Taking into consideration the fact that each porter was strictly limited by Newland and Tarleton to carrying no more than a total of sixty pounds, and that each of these porters needed to be fed and sheltered, too, Akeley's total number of porters is far from excessive.

The British colonial officials were strict about charging fees for the privilege of taking game animals, and Roosevelt was hardly exempt from needing a hunting license. Nevertheless, a standard license allowed each shooter an abundance of game, including two each of buffalo, rhinoceros, and hippopotamus. In addition, a hunter could take six oryx, four waterbuck, four lesser kudu, more than twenty zebra, and one each of the greater kudu and eland, in addition to dozens more assorted antelope.

Such permissive bag limits were alarming even to some of the British sport hunting elites, and already some White hunters were calling for the curtailment of the slaughter. Dubbing themselves the "penitent butchers," they had done the math and determined that the scale of their hunting was unsustainable. Yet there were others who pointed to the absurdity of keeping the land in pristine condition merely for the benefit of wildlife; the colonial government wished to clear out all the large animals as part of a deliberate effort to ready the land for settlement by White farmers. The hard reality was that much of the land comprising British East Africa would soon be transformed, and Roosevelt had consciously launched his expedition in the spirit of documenting its spectacular fauna while it was still possible.

Arriving in Nairobi, Akeley was handed a letter from Roosevelt saying that he hoped to rendezvous with him somewhere on the Uasin Gishu plateau, a rather desolate expanse of land more than a hundred miles to the west. The meeting would be good publicity for Akeley, who had to raise a fair amount of the money for his own expeditions. As it was, Akeley was hosting two of his sponsors in the field—John T. McCutcheon and Fred Stephenson. Stephenson was an experienced big-game hunter from Minnesota who was willing to subsidize part of the expedition just for the chance to hunt with Akeley; J. T. McCutcheon was a well-known cartoonist for the *Chicago Tribune*. Together, the two men would keep Akeley's expedition flush with money and in the news.

While Akeley's main objective for the 1909 American Museum expedition was to secure a big bull elephant as the centerpiece for his exhibit, he spent his first five weeks on the Athi Plains, where nary an elephant could be found. Situated just outside Nairobi, the plains offered a diversity of game in an environment that was neither too challenging nor too far from the city, in the event of unforeseen problems. Roosevelt's own safari had started out making one of their first camps here, it being a customary way for a new expedition to work out the kinks of their operation and get into the rhythm of the hunt.

On the Athi Plains, Akeley guided McCutcheon and Stephenson on a number of lion hunts, although these were unsuccessful at first. Hardly a sport hunter himself, Akeley was more devoted to shooting motion picture photography, and he especially wanted to film a rhinoceros at full charge. Flanked by McCutcheon and Stephenson—their rifles cocked and ready—Akeley provoked many of these animals to charge, with the two shooters firing grazing shots to "turn" any animals that came in too close.

Days spent hunting lions and rhinos were followed by evenings with drinks before a fire, and it was during one of these sundowners that talk turned to monkeys. J. T. thought they were dirty animals, but Delia disagreed, and she was intent on proving him wrong. The next day Delia made what would turn out to be a life-changing decision—she trapped a monkey. It was a young female vervet monkey, which Bill, their former "tent boy" who was now thirteen, had helped her capture in a basket baited with some corn. She had originally intended to release the animal rather quickly, after satisfying her curiosity about it, but her maternal instincts immediately kicked in. Gazing into the monkey's big brown eyes, she found herself irrevocably drawn to the animal. It wasn't long before the vervet had a name, and thumbing her nose at McCutcheon, Delia called her little monkey J. T. Jr.

Innocent though her intentions may have been at the time, the monkey quickly habituated, and try as she did to release the animal, she could never bring herself to do it. She also made excuses, claiming that she was engaged in a scientific study of her captive's behavior. The object of her maternal energies, the monkey began acting like a spoiled child. Together, Delia and J. T. Jr. started taking picnics together, and in the evening they sometimes both climbed trees to watch the African sunsets. Soon J. T. Jr. was sleeping with Delia in her bed at night.

Delia outfitted J. T. Jr. with her own personal valet, a young Swahili boy named Ali, whom she dressed in a smart khaki suit and red fez. Ali would hold an umbrella over the monkey during long marches, and he collected fresh flowers to keep her amused. J. T. Jr. wore a silver collar engraved with her name, and when they needed to take the train, she traveled in the same car as Carl and Delia on a child's boarding pass. Carl grew more than a little resentful toward the monkey as she got more and more between him and his wife.

The expedition moved on to Mt. Kenya, where Akeley hoped to find his big tusker. He was excited to be back on the mountain where he and Delia had shot elephants before, and they visited their old camp on the mountain overlooking the farms below. Some of their previous guides showed up to offer their services, informing them that elephants were still abundant. Day after day they hunted, and although they saw plenty of elephants, none were quite big enough. Akeley grew anxious, wondering if the kind of big tusker he was looking for still existed. He and Delia climbed all the way up to the glaciers at the top of the mountain, wondering if the elephants were hiding up there, but J. T. Jr. succumbed to altitude sickness and had to be taken back down. It was just as well because of the fast-approaching date of the planned rendezvous with Roosevelt.

Arriving on the edge of the Uasin Gishu plateau at the beginning of November, Akeley was greeted by a messenger with a note from Roosevelt. It described his general whereabouts, but it was of limited value because the man was a moving target. Still, Akeley reckoned Roosevelt was probably somewhere three days' march to the west of him on the Nzoia River. The next morning, Akeley spotted a dust cloud in the distance, and peering through his army field glasses, he confirmed that it was a large safari on the move. The expedition was so large that it could only be the Smithsonian Roosevelt Expedition, and Akeley moved to intersect its path.

Relieved to have found Roosevelt, Akeley brought him back to his camp to meet Delia, who promptly introduced the ex-president to her little monkey. They all had lunch together, during which time Roosevelt talked with "the freedom of one who was glad to see some American friends in the wilderness." Their talk soon turned to elephants, and their plan for Roosevelt to shoot at least one cow for the Akeleys' exhibit. In fact, Roosevelt had just seen a nice herd of elephants a few hours before, he told the group, and it was agreed that they would go after them the next morning.

They found the herd of eight cows and calves resting under an acacia tree. Watching from behind an anthill, Akeley pointed out the one cow he wanted for his group. He expected Roosevelt to shoot from where he stood, but instead he walked straight toward the elephants, which was a particularly risky move. Halfway across the open space, the hunted animal spread her ears, curled her trunk, and charged with an angry squeal. Roosevelt shot and the elephant went to her knees, but she got up, and then the whole herd came toward them, bellowing and screaming. Roosevelt fired again and the cow went down for good, but the others kept coming. Akeley and Kermit had to keep shooting, dropping two more cows and a young calf. In the span of a day, the meeting of Roosevelt and Akeley was over, and four elephants lay dead.

Akeley now faced the tremendous task of skinning half a herd of elephants before they spoiled under the blazing sun. James Clark had recently joined up with his expedition, and Akeley sent word for him to come with the salt they needed to preserve the hides at once. But Clark got lost trying to find him, and had to spend the night on the open plain fending off the rhinos that kept charging his campfire. When Clark finally arrived on the scene of the carnage the next day, he was amazed to see how Akeley and his men had managed to skin all four elephants in the night, but they nearly lost their lives doing so. A brushfire had swept down upon them, fanned by strong winds, and it was only by lighting backfires that they kept from being encircled and burned.

Still searching for his prized tusker, Akeley parted ways with Roosevelt to try his luck on Mt. Elgon, the fourteen-thousand-foot extinct volcano on the Uganda-Kenya border. Here they hunted until the end of the year, when Fred and J. T. had to return to Nairobi. This left Carl and Delia alone to continue searching for that perfect bull elephant, which by now Akeley was referring to as his Moby Dick.

From Mt. Elgon, Carl and Delia moved into Uganda, where they spent several months hunting in the Budongo Forest. In the hot and wet climate, Carl was often sick with dysentery and fever. On better days, he would make a feeble effort to hunt, but he was eventually forced back to the Uasin Gishu, where in the cool dry highlands he began to recover. Then one day, "in a reckless moment," Carl and Delia decided to return to Mt. Kenya. They wanted to climb to the top of the mountain, which was something they never had the time for on any of their previous journeys.

Arriving in June, they made their base camp in a village on the southwest side of the peak, and together with forty porters, they proceeded to cut a trail to the top. They went through the bamboo of the middle elevations, and the peat bogs above the tree line, until finally they reached the ice fields somewhere under seventeen thousand feet. As Delia later recalled it, "We quenched our thirst with icy water from rock pools at the base of lovely waterfalls. We slept nightly on a bed of cedar boughs which were often laid over a carpet of violets, and we were awakened in the morning by the trumpeting of elephants." It was "a glorious adventure."

Heading back down the mountain, they returned to their camp in the village. There Akeley developed the pictures he had taken in the forest only to discover that many of them did not turn out. He needed good reference photos for his elephant exhibit, which he planned to show in a forest of bamboo, and so Akeley decided to make another trip up the mountain. Seeing her husband off, Delia followed the departing safari up the trail for a little while before returning to the village, hardly suspecting that something terrible was about to happen. Three days later, two men from Akeley's party came back down the mountain just before sundown. When Delia saw them, she thought that maybe Carl had finally gotten his elephant.

Having gone up the mountain to retake photographs, Akeley nonetheless always carried his elephant gun, and encountering some fresh elephant spoor, he decided to turn his photographic trip into a hunt. He had been stalking a particularly large bull in the early dawn mists. It was cold, and his hands were numb, so he stopped momentarily to warm them. Resting his rifle against his stomach, he rubbed some feeling back into his icy fingers. Suddenly, a cold sweat on his back directed him to danger from behind. He grabbed his rifle and swung around. An angry bull elephant was crashing through the brush directly toward him. He tried to shoot but only fumbled with the trigger. Everything had happened so fast. In an instant the elephant was upon him.

Akeley tossed his gun aside. He had long visualized what he would do in this situation. He faced the elephant head-on and grabbed one tusk, and then he swung his body between that one tusk and the other so that at least he would not be gored to death. The enraged bull, with Akeley trapped between the tusks, forced both tusks deep down into the soft ground. Pressing down into the earth, the bull was intent on crushing Akeley to death with its massive head.

Akeley saw his "merciless little eye gleaming revenge," close to his own as the animal pushed harder into the earth, until something underground, either a rock or a root, prevented the elephant from completely crushing him. He heard a "wheezy grunt" as, one by one, his own ribs cracked. Just then an excruciating pain overcame him and he passed out, but the elephant was not done with him. Although he appeared dead, the bull elephant pulled back from Akeley's limp body, and in one last furious act whipped him in the face with his trunk, breaking his nose, rendering a nasty gash in his forehead, and tearing away a part of Akeley's cheek to expose the molars in his jaw. Just as soon as the elephant was done with Akeley, it turned on his men, who scattered through the forest while the beast chased after them, trumpeting wildly with anger.

When his men finally mustered the courage to return to the scene, they thought for sure that Akeley was dead, and they did not want to touch him. It was dark before Akeley finally regained consciousness, as he took in the blurred sight of his men standing before a fire in the forest clearing. Dimly, he could make out their forms, but then slipped back into oblivion only to wake again, his body shivering. Slowly he remembered parts of what had happened that morning, and mustering his strength, he called out.

At last realizing he was alive, his men no longer feared touching him. They moved him closer to the fire, and he regained some of his senses. They had already sent a couple of runners down the mountain to inform Delia, but she was some three thousand feet below them, and it being dark, they were unlikely to return anytime soon. Finally gathering the strength to speak, he asked for his wife and some whiskey before ordering his men to fire off location shots at regular intervals. He could only hope that Delia was already trying to find him.

The two runners who had been sent down to find Delia were too terrified to approach her. Casually wandering into her camp at sundown—close to ten hours after the mauling—they milled about not knowing what to do. Eventually they found Bill, who sheepishly broke the news. At first Delia was shocked, but then she sprang into action. She chose twenty men to accompany her on a rescue mission up the mountain. The sun had already set, but she could not afford to wait until dawn. She assembled gear—tents, supplies, and medicine—and then using some lengths of cloth they had for barter, she proceeded to stitch together a crude stretcher, sewing feverishly by the light of a dim lantern on the floor of her tent until midnight.

A chilly rain came down, and hyenas prowled outside the perimeter of the camp. Delia sent the camp guard to round up her men, but only Bill appeared. The men were in an "ugly mood," he said, adding that they were threatening to kill her and leave her body for the hyenas. They were deathly afraid to go into the jungle at night. Feeling helpless, Delia fell into a rage. She snapped at Bill, telling him he would be better off staying in camp taking care of her pet monkey, and then she grabbed her rifle and confronted her staff. "Twenty primitive, superstitious men with murder in their hearts and the cold, black night against me," she later wrote of that moment. They stood at an impasse, and just as Delia was about to speak, a shrieking of a hyena pierced the night. Whether out of fear or sheer terror, all she could do was point her rifle and laugh. It was a nervous laugh, but then one of the men standing before her laughed, too, and then several others. Soon the tension was relieved, and the men formed a line and started marching into the night, led by the fearless Delia on a quest to rescue Akeley.

After the elephant attack, Akeley spent three months recovering in camp, and it was during this period of recovery that an important thing happened. While he lay on his cot, his forced stillness allowed him the luxury of some serious daydreaming. In these hazy interludes, as he drifted in and out of pain, he created in his mind a wonderful monument to Africa. He envisioned his Africa Hall, and it would become his obsession for the rest of his life.

CHAPTER TEN

Terra Firma

Roy Chapman Andrews returned from Korea determined to move his life in a new direction. It was 1912, and he was done studying whales. Actually, it had never been his plan to study marine mammals in the first place. He only fell into it by happenchance when he was ordered to salvage that northern right whale beached at Amagansett. Digging that skeleton out of the frigid surf established him as a cetologist. He really had no choice in the matter because he was so new to the museum. He had to show his enthusiasm for whatever tasks came his way, but he did not care to have the stench of rancid whale blubber clinging to him forever.

Although proud to have built up an impressive collection of whale skeletons, Andrews had gone to the American Museum intent on becoming an explorer on land. Reminded of this after his jaunt through Korea, he was determined at the age of twenty-eight to refocus his priorities. Terra firma was what Andrews desired, and he knew he would be happiest traipsing across Asia—"the lure of lands, the thrill of the unknown, the desire to know what lay over the next hill! Central Asia was the magnet which drew me irresistibly."

Perhaps also enticing Andrews were some of his liaisons back in Japan, for despite all the invitations from young women in New York, Roy was smitten with a girl in Japan. Writing to a friend in Yokohama in February 1913, he instructed him to use an enclosed check to purchase a new kimono for his "best girl." The garment was custom-made, "light blue embroidered in Wisteria," the assisting friend explained. "I am sorry to hear that you are stricken so badly," he added. "I remember the yarns you used to spin to me about some other dear little girlie."

Along with his whale studies, Andrews also abandoned any hope of finishing his doctoral degree. He didn't have time. "I have never been quite so busy in my life I think as since my return from this trip," he complained. Just three weeks after he got back from Korea, his calendar was already filled with speaking engagements, for which he charged the standard fee of $100 per lecture. He decided to finish his schooling at Columbia with a master of arts degree. He had taken all the necessary classes, including Osborn's "Mammals Living and Fossil," and for a thesis he chose to cobble something together from his most recent work on gray whales.

For the first half of 1913, Andrews worked on little else but finishing his degree. He graduated in June, just a few weeks before his last round of whale work. The museum had asked him to sail aboard the schooner *Adventress* in an attempt to secure a bowhead whale—the only species of great whale still absent from the AMNH collection. The trip up to Alaska, however, proved to be something more of a pleasure cruise for the millionaires who were his sponsors. They were never really serious about letting Andrews get so close to whales, and as if to end this last chapter of his life at sea, Andrews memorialized his whale-hunting career by publishing a popular book describing his nautical adventures, *Whale Hunting with Gun and Camera.*

Starting his life afresh in 1914, Andrews enjoyed the bubbly life of New York society. With his magnetic personality, he was invited to endless receptions, banquets, and lectures. Always debonair, Andrews was sought out by the city's most prominent socialites, and was frequently seen in the company of beautiful women. Young and handsome, despite his prematurely receding hairline, Andrews had the reputation of being a ladies' man, and so everyone was stunned when he announced his engagement to be married later that same year.

Yvette Borup was the spirited sister of Roy's late friend George Borup, an Arctic explorer who had died in an accidental drowning while Andrews was in Korea. The daughter of a well-traveled army officer, she had been born in Paris and was raised a debutante in the upper echelons of Parisian society. Beautiful and petite, with chestnut hair and brown eyes, she made Europe her playground, and had studied ballet and drama at the Paris Conservatory. She was fluent in French, German, and English, and after the family moved to Germany, she became friendly with Princess Victoria Louise and was a frequent guest at the German court.

Roy and Yvette were married on October 7, 1914, after which they took a deer-hunting honeymoon in the Adirondacks, where the groom bagged a total of three. Returning in November, they settled into a comfortable house in the quaint upscale community of Lawrence Park, just north of New York City. A brief period of domestic life ensued, but it wasn't long before Andrews was looking for an excuse to go back abroad. Needing a justification to return to Asia, he ultimately pandered to the needs of the museum's president.

Osborn had for a long time been promoting the idea of central Asia as "the birthplace of primitive humans" and the source of much of the animal life found in the Northern Hemisphere. He noted the similarities between the faunas of Europe and western North America, and reasoned that the area in-between—central Asia—had to be the place of origin for all these mammals, both living and fossil. While recognizing that others thought Africa a more likely source, Osborn carefully refuted this theory on the grounds that only certain highly specialized forms—obscure species of gliding rodents, for example—showed any evidence of having originated in Africa, and that all the more advanced orders of mammals appeared to have evolved where they currently resided, in the north.

Extending this idea to humans, Osborn called northeastern Asia the "Cradle of Mankind," and predicted that the ancient ancestors of modern humans would be found there soon enough, if only someone would make the effort to look. Central Asia remained virtually unexplored for fossils, and in 1900 Osborn published an explicit call for more paleontology work in the region, writing that "here is a region for explorers." More than a decade later, Andrews thought he would answer Osborn's call.

Andrews wanted to get back into the field, and hunting fossils seemed the perfect justification. As for Osborn, he just wanted someone to find proof for what he had been saying all along—that Asia was the "Garden of Eden," and the place of origin of modern European man. Andrews carefully considered the concept, turning all its details over in his mind before cautiously approaching Osborn with his plan. He proposed to launch a reconnaissance of the southern edge of the central Asian plateau along the Tibetan frontier. It was a wild and mountainous region, and its fauna was virtually unknown. Andrews proposed this first expedition as being mostly zoological in nature. His goal was to familiarize himself with the land and to collect mammals for his studies of the whole region.

Osborn was enthusiastic, but he worried about finances. The expedition would cost $15,000, but the museum could not even afford to pay half that amount. In the end, it was Andrews's engaging personality that made the trip possible, and he secured all the money he needed in just two months. By the beginning of 1916, preparations were complete for what the museum officially designated as the Asiatic Zoological Expedition.

Andrews would lead the expedition, with his new wife Yvette serving as official photographer. To help with collecting and preserving the zoological specimens that were the object of their mission, they would hire Edmund Heller, the peripatetic naturalist known for the efficiency with which he could trap and stuff mice. He had previously been on ex-president Roosevelt's expedition, and would meet up with the expedition in China.

On March 28, 1916, Roy Chapman Andrews and Yvette sailed from San Francisco aboard the *Tenyo Maru* for Japan. "We went off to the accompaniment of popping flashlight bulbs and screaming headlines," Andrews recalled. They were real celebrities, in part because one of their preliminary objectives had been so sensationalized in the newspapers. They were to hunt a so-called blue tiger of unusually dark coloration in the jungles of south China. The tiger was real, and had been reported by a well-known "shooting missionary" named Harry Caldwell as being a man-eater. Andrews hunted the animal for weeks, chasing reports of it from village to village, and although he got at least one fleeting view of the tiger, he never got off a shot.

Moving on to Hanoi, in what was the French colony of Tonkin, the expedition reorganized the four thousand pounds of baggage they needed to conduct their expedition before taking a train up the valley of the Red River to Kunming, the capital of Yunnan Province, China. Here they purchased mules and began their long trek along the same mountain path that Marco Polo had followed centuries before. "It was a highway which wound over mountain peaks, down into valleys, across rivers on swinging rope bridges and finally reached the jungle-filled plains of Burma and the Irrawaddy River," Andrews wrote. While on the path they camped in old temples, many of them half ruined, but at one point they ventured far north to the border of Tibet so that Andrews could see for himself "where wild aboriginal tribes lived in secluded mountain valleys."

Wherever the expedition went, they searched for animals, "for this was a zoological expedition pure and simple for the purpose of bringing back to the American Museum a cross section of the animal life of this little known region," Andrews reminded himself. One of their objectives was Snow Mountain, which rose twenty thousand feet above sea level. "Below the summit in a grassy meadow beside a stream of green snow water, our tents were pitched just at the edge of the spruce forest," Andrews wrote, "then we climbed to the grassy slope above timber line to set a hundred traps in the runways of meadow voles and under logs and stumps in the forest." Unaccustomed to the altitude, Andrews's heart pounded like a hammer, and he could move only at a slow walk.

In this wild country along the Tibetan frontier, Andrews hunted serow, goral, muntjac, and "other strange animals" of the deer and mountain goat families. "Every mountain range brought us into new valleys occupied by strange aboriginal people," he remarked. The land was rugged, and full of species that had been isolated for millennia. *Vicariance* is the word zoologists use to describe how the impassability of deep gorges, swift rivers, and high mountain ranges can lead to the isolation of animal populations. Unable to escape the bounds of the lands within which they are enclosed, these ancient lineages of animals evolve in isolation, kept pure by the ruggedness of the terrain.

Andrews was on the lookout for isolated populations of ancient humans, too, and he believed he found them "hidden away deep in a secluded valley." It was a Lolo village, and after examining some of its inhabitants, he described them as "fine, tall fellows." They had "long heads, high-bridged noses, and thin lips and faces almost Caucasian in type." Andrews hoped to describe how the very remoteness and complexity of the land made it a cradle for all kinds of newly evolved species, including humans. The animals he collected would provide a baseline of support for Osborn's concept that the high plateau of Asia was the place where the ancestors of modern European man originated.

From Tibet, the expedition crossed the Mekong River gorge and headed southward into "the steaming tropics of the Burma border . . . a country as different from that we had left as Cuba is from Alaska." They had spent nine months wandering over hundreds of miles of rugged terrain, and traversing altitudes from fourteen hundred to fifteen thousand feet above sea level. Along the way they had amassed "the biggest collection ever taken out of Asia on a single expedition," which in the end comprised a total of forty-one cases of specimens loaded onto thirty mules. The entire bounty had to be carried with them the whole time they were in the field, there being no way to send them ahead. Surveying the contents of all these boxes while decamped in northern Burma, Andrews was gratified to note that they included some 2,100 mammals, 800 birds, 200 reptiles and amphibians, and hundreds of Yvette's photographs and thousands of feet of film.

Of great importance to Andrews was the fact that they had made important zoological collections in one of the most biogeographically complex and zoologically diverse parts of Asia. And as they would later discover when studying their meticulously labeled specimens back at the museum, their efforts showed how almost every altitudinal zone of every mountain range they had sampled had its own unique species composition. Nearly every ridgetop and every valley was home to unique species that occurred nowhere else. So complex was the topography, and so ancient the forests, that they seemed to be passing through a laboratory of evolution much like that which Darwin had encountered when he explored the various islands of the Galápagos. Surely this was the place to elucidate the history of the evolution of mammals.

Decamping in Burma, Andrews realized that he might not be able to conclude his work as he had planned. After months of isolation in the interior, he was just hearing the news of America's entry into the Great War, an event that seriously hampered his ability to ship both his specimens as well as Yvette and himself home. Adding to his anxiety was the fact that Yvette was now seven months pregnant. The clock ticking, they had to first make their way to Rangoon, from where they had to cross the Bay of Bengal to Calcutta on the east coast of India, only to travel overland across the subcontinent just to get to Bombay. There they waited for three weeks for a ship that would take them back east across the Bay of Bengal to Singapore so they could finally make their way across the Pacific to the West Coast of the United States by way of Hong Kong and Japan. Roy and Yvette arrived in New York on October 1, 1917, exactly four months after the official conclusion of their yearlong collecting expedition. Two months after their return, on December 26, Yvette gave birth to a son, George Borup Andrews.

Soon after, Andrews went to Washington to call on an acquaintance, Newton D. Baker, the secretary of war. He wanted to volunteer his services in France, "wishing desperately," he said, "to be part of the action." The secretary declined, urging Andrews that he would be more useful to the war effort in the army's intelligence corps. Andrews was being offered a desk job in Washington, which was hardly what he was hoping for. Disheartened, Andrews skulked off to the Cosmos Club for lunch. There he was "sitting disconsolately at a small table," he recalled, when he was spotted by a friend, Charles Sheldon, a well-known big-game hunter affiliated with the American Museum. Sheldon himself was serving in naval intelligence, and what is more, he was eager to recruit Andrews to spy for the navy in the Far East.

Andrews signed some papers and took his oath of allegiance in Washington on June 10, 1918. A week later he was on his way back to Peking, where he was to establish his base of operations under cover of carrying out zoological collections for the American Museum. Given the code name "Reynolds" and a letter of introduction written in invisible ink, Andrews arrived in Peking to find it "a city of intrigue." All foreigners, especially newcomers, were presumed to be secret agents, as many of them undoubtedly were.

Little is known of what exactly "Reynolds" did for the navy at the edge of a sea of sand, but he apparently made several horseback treks across the north of China and into Manchuria. More presciently, he also made a couple of automobile trips across the Mongolian plain to the capital city of Urga. According to Andrews's biographer, recently declassified documents confirm that Andrews was one of many civilian informants, operating under various guises, whose job it was to gather data on a wide range of subjects for use in formulating American policies in eastern Asia. Andrews, for example, filed reports on communication and rail facilities, troop movements, industrial output, armaments, and on any evidence of foreign—and especially Japanese—intervention in China and Manchuria.

Aside from these intrigues, Andrews used his official cover as a museum mammalogist to traverse the Gobi Desert in order to scope it out for future scientific work. The area offered "undreamed-of possibilities for testing Osborn's idea regarding mammalian evolution," and from the moment he passed through the Great Wall at Kalgan and set foot in Mongolia on his first reconnaissance trip in August 1918, he was smitten. He described the land as "cut and slashed by the knives of wind and frost and rain," and felt certain that he would one day return to this land of "ravines, and gullies, painted in rainbow colors."

All through his wartime service in Asia, Andrews dreamed of launching what he would call the Second Asiatic Expedition. He envisioned it as the next phase of the concept he proposed to Osborn in 1915, and its objective would be to collect mammals and birds in northern Mongolia. When the war finally ended, Andrews did not even bother to return to the United States, instead remaining in Peking. He rented a secluded house in a walled compound near the city's legation district with the intention of resuming museum explorations in the region. Yvette and George, who was now nine months old, joined him in Peking toward the end of September, while Andrews set about arranging his new expedition entirely by cables and letters to the museum. Osborn gave his wholehearted support, agreeing to provide half the project's modest budget, estimated by Andrews to be about $7,500, with the balance paid by a wealthy benefactor.

The Second Asiatic Expedition of the AMNH began in February 1919. Andrews joined his old pal Charles Coltman, who operated trading stations in Kalgan and Urga, and then secured automobiles for the journey to the Mongolian capital, where the expedition would officially begin. They departed on May 17 with three cars loaded up with gear, and drove along the well-worn gravel caravan trail that extended roughly seven hundred miles between Kalgan and Urga. In addition to Andrews and Yvette, the party included Charles Coltman and his wife, and two Chinese taxidermists, Chen and Kang, along with a cook known as Wu. A soldier named Owen hired by Coltman served as a driver for one of the cars, and they were also joined by a Mr. and Mrs. Ted MacCallie, friends of the Coltmans.

Unlike Andrews's earlier expeditions, the whole affair had the feeling of a sporty outing, with Wu's excellent cooking and an ample supply of liquor. Everyone was in a jubilant mood, and Andrews was especially thrilled to be back in the field with Yvette, little George having been left behind with a Swiss nanny in Peking. He described the trip as "une belle excursion" and referred to his traveling companions as "the Grouchless Gang." Every few miles Andrews and Coltman stopped to shoot gophers, yellow marmots, rabbits, wolves, and antelope for the museum collection. They collected birds, too—geese, mallards, sheldrakes, teals, and cranes. The ducks in particular served double duty as meals, as Wu improvised a makeshift oven out of a gasoline can. Entranced by her first glimpse of Mongolia, Yvette photographed wildlife, nomad encampments, and landscapes, as well as lamaseries and passing caravans, until at last they reached Urga, the "City of the Living God."

Situated in northeastern Mongolia, roughly 160 miles below the Russian border, the scenery was reminiscent of a frontier town in the American West. From here the members of the Second Asiatic Expedition replaced their cars with horses and carts. Their destination was a district some three hundred miles southwest of Urga that was supposed to be full of game, but they encountered very little of interest. Returning to Urga on June 16, they next turned their attention to the eastern plains, where they spent two months close to the Russian border. By September it was getting cool, and they were back in Peking on the first day of October.

Although small in scale, the Second Asiatic Expedition of the AMNH returned with more than one thousand small mammals, as well as elk, moose, antelope, wild boar, tiger, and a record-sized mountain sheep. "I had learned much about the country and its ways," Andrews commented, "talked with wandering Mongols about the far western desert, studied the physical problems of transport and maintenance in the arid reaches of the Gobi. All I learned made me more certain that this was the chosen spot in Central Asia . . . the place where I could stake all to lose or win on a single play." Indeed, the Second Asiatic Expedition was reconnaissance for much greater things to come.

PART III

MAD DASHES

CHAPTER ELEVEN

The Great Race

In the spring of 1916—and while men were fighting and dying in the trenches of war-torn Europe—Henry Fairfield Osborn quietly paged through a thick manuscript at his desk. Its subject seemed especially timely in light of all the bloodshed overseas. Written by his friend Madison Grant, *The Passing of the Great Race* was as much a retelling of European history as it was a warning of the looming decline of the so-called Nordics. Easily recognized by their fair hair and light eyes, the Nordics were supposed to be a superior race, but if Grant was to be believed, they were also an endangered species.

The opening passages of Grant's book made it clear that he wished to explain European history in terms of race. "The great lesson of the science of race," Grant explained, was that it was about so much more than just one's physical characteristics—the shape of the head or breadth of the nose—because along with these came equally immutable spiritual impulses, such as courage and perseverance. According to Grant, race was the basis for "all the phenomena of modern society." His book was a sweeping overview of Western history from the perspective of a scientific racist, and it retold the history of mankind as a series of migrations and conquests. To Grant,

Europe was a battleground of races vying for superiority. It was survival of the fittest, and at least according to Grant, it was the Nordics who had come out on top.

Divided into two parts, Grant's book covered in the first section the basic tenets of scientific racism, detailing the specific physical characteristics most useful for recognizing each race—everything from hair color and eye color, to the slope of the forehead and overall stature. Writing in an erudite tone, Grant gives the book a patina of scientific credibility, despite his weakness for digressing into rants about the growing number of non-Nordic immigrants in America. He even complained of an inferior kind of Nordic hailing from southwest Norway that he referred to as "dark Norwegians" on account of their non-blond status. "These dark Norwegians are regarded as somewhat inferior socially by their Nordic countrymen," Grant explained, adding that "perhaps as a result of this disability, a disproportionately large number of Norwegian immigrants to America are of this type." In chapter after chapter, Madison Grant was adamant that if anything was to be learned from the history of Europe, it was that America should remain a Nordic-majority society.

The second part of the book surveyed European prehistory from the beginning of the Stone Age. Drawing on the writings of others, William Ripley among them, Grant described the Nordic, Alpine, and Mediterranean races of Europe. Of these, Grant explained how the Nordics still resided where they had first evolved—in the forests and steppes of northern Europe—and of how the other two races were interlopers. The Alpines, with their stocky build and more rounded heads, had come from Southwestern Asia to occupy the mountainous terrain of eastern and central Europe, Grant explained. The Mediterraneans, on the other hand, with their swarthy skin and broad noses, migrated to southern and western Europe from North Africa. Throughout the pages of his discourse, pullout maps and charts add to the feeling of scholarly credibility. Readers could plainly see for themselves a map showing the "Expansion of the Pre-Teutonic Nordics" in the centuries before Christ, or the "Present Distributions of European Races," and feel assured that it was all incontrovertible fact.

In addition to detailing all the physical differences between these three supposed races, Grant claimed that each was endowed with specific mental traits, too. "Moral, intellectual, and spiritual attributes are as persistent as physical characters and are transmitted unchanged from generation to generation," he wrote. Noting that the typical British sailor was "always a blond," he went on to explain how this fact would indicate that "nomadism as well as love of war and adventure are Nordic characteristics." He even went on to show how the founders of the United States were Nordics—"the white man par excellence"—a point made, perhaps, because Grant traced his own ancestry to some of the founders of America.

Although focused on European racial history, the book was written for an American audience, and in describing the rise and fall of European peoples, Grant made it plain that it was an object lesson for what could happen in the United States. He painted a picture of the American Nordics as standing on the brink of extinction—a lordly race about to be snuffed out—and he was adamant that something needed to be done, if only to uphold his own social status. The solution, Grant believed, was to be found in eugenics.

As a set of practices aimed at improving the genetic quality of human populations, the pseudoscience of eugenics emerged in the late nineteenth century thanks to Francis Galton. Inspired by the work of his famous cousin—Charles Darwin—Galton sought to improve human populations through selective breeding. To Galton, desirable human qualities were a matter of genetics, with a person's upbringing or living conditions having little to do with their success in life and status in society. Galton believed that personality traits—intelligence or competitiveness on the one hand, or a tendency toward mental illness or criminality on the other—were just as heritable as physical characteristics. He based this claim on his own groundbreaking advances in statistics. Galton is credited with inventing the fundamentals of regression and correlation, and he used these methods to make sweeping statements about society. While recognizing that one could certainly improve the character of any individual through education and social welfare, Galton was quick to point out that such gains could not be passed on to the person's offspring. Each generation of less-well-endowed individuals would have to be educated from the same lowly starting point as every other member of the lineage, and at great expense to society.

Henry Fairfield Osborn agreed with Galton's overall line of thinking, and in the preface to Grant's book, he wrote of how he felt that race played a crucial role in human history—"Race implies heredity and heredity implies all the moral, social and intellectual characteristics and traits which are the spring of politics and government." Blending patriotism and eugenics, he advocated for the "conservation of the race which has given us the true spirit of Americanism," and added that this way of thinking was "not a matter of racial pride or of racial prejudice" but rather "a matter of love of country." Deploring anything less as ignorant sentimentalism, Osborn ended his preface with a most damning statement: "If I were asked: What is the greatest danger which threatens the American republic to-day? I would certainly reply: The gradual dying out among our people of those hereditary traits through which the principles of our religious, political and social foundations were laid down and their insidious replacement by traits of less noble character."

Osborn was the perfect man to review Madison Grant's book. He had just the year before published *Men of the Old Stone Age* (1915), and saw *The Passing of the Great Race* as an extension of his own work. But whereas Osborn's book told the story of human evolution, Grant's attempted to explain how the end results of human evolution applied to current generations. Thus, Osborn's attempt at understanding the history of human evolution led to the application of that knowledge toward promoting a social agenda.

As a eugenicist, Osborn held that the natural process of evolution

Henry Fairfield Osborn as a young Princeton professor.

Albert S. Bickmore was determined to found the American Museum of Natural History in New York City.

The AMNH as it appeared when Osborn accepted a position as its first curator of paleontology.

Osborn as a rising star in the leadership of the AMNH.

Carl Akeley resting with his guides while on an expedition for the Field Museum in Somalia, 1895.

Delia Akeley with the skull and tusks of the record elephant she shot on Mt. Kenya for the Field Museum.

Under Osborn's leadership, the AMNH saw its greatest expansion.

Enamored with the Far East, Roy Chapman Andrews immersed himself in many aspects of Japanese life and is here shown wearing a kimono.

Andrews was often portrayed as a role model of manliness.

Madison Grant helped save the giant redwood trees and the American bison from extinction. He founded the New York Zoological Society and Bronx Zoo and was the author of *The Passing of the Great Race*—an influential treatise on scientific racism.

This painting of a Neanderthal family is one of nine large murals commissioned from Charles Knight for Osborn's Hall of the Age of Man.

Osborn at the peak of his power at the AMNH.

Delia with J. T. Jr. on her shoulder looking through binoculars in Africa, 1910.

Andrews made effective use of caravans of camels to keep his expedition supplied while traversing the Gobi Desert with automobiles.

Akeley with a completed bull elephant that would form the centerpiece of his herd of elephants in Africa Hall.

Andrews and his camel caravan leader, Merin, in the Gobi Desert.

Looking at the faces of the gorillas he had shot for his exhibit, Akeley felt like a murderer. Here he contemplates a plaster "death mask" used as a reference for his taxidermy work.

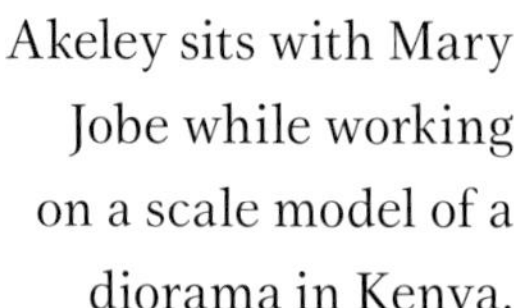

Akeley sits with Mary Jobe while working on a scale model of a diorama in Kenya.

Looking rather stylish, Osborn joined the Central Asiatic Expedition in 1923.

Working in plein air, artists paint background studies for one of Akeley's dioramas.

Akeley not long before his death while on expedition in the eastern Congo.

Akeley's Africa Hall was completed after his death and is today considered one of the great masterpieces of museum taxidermy exhibits.

Akeley was buried near the site depicted in his gorilla diorama, described by him as the most beautiful place in the world.

Osborn in December 1932, just months before his death. In the end, his pseudoscientific ideas were widely discredited.

could be directed through deliberate selective actions. He believed that by encouraging certain favored individuals to have more children, he could enhance the human species. Madison Grant, however, took a more extreme view, and indeed, he helped swing the eugenics movement in a far more dangerous direction. Prior to Grant, the movement was focused more on unfit individuals, not on inferior races. The original goal of the eugenicists was to raise the hereditary endowment of all mankind, with the hope that all the races might eventually reach the intellectual level of the upper classes. Madison Grant, on the other hand, was instrumental in transforming eugenics to where it was at war with entire groups of people deemed racially unfit. What was at first an idea of selective breeding within human races became a program for the elimination of all but his most favored races.

In radicalizing eugenics, Grant went so far as to argue for the controlled breeding of humans to remove degenerate traits, even if it required an abandonment of such democratic ideas as the "brotherhood of man." He advocated for halting the arrival of new immigrants, and even sought to establish ghettos and forced sterilization for the "undesirables" already in America. In this way, Grant helped shape the three basic tenets of the most ardent eugenicists for dealing with perceived biological threats: first, keep out as many immigrants as possible; second, segregate undesirables already here to keep them from mixing with the native population; and third, sterilize undesirables as necessary so they could no longer breed their kind.

More than just promoting a hateful agenda, what Grant achieved with the publication of his book was the amalgamation of several distinct scientific disciplines—everything from paleoanthropology and genetics to sociology and wildlife management—into what we would today call scientific racism. At the most basic level, scientific racism adhered to three basic principles: (1) that the human species is divided into biologically distinct races, and that these were hierarchical, with the Nordics at the top; (2) that along with the defining physical characteristics of a race came certain moral, intellectual, and behavioral traits that were inherited, and not the result of one's environment; and (3) that the mixing of races led to a reversion to the more primitive type, and that measures needed to be taken to prevent the degradation of the superior race.

The Passing of the Great Race went on sale in October 1916, but it garnered little attention at first. Everyone was preoccupied with the ongoing First World War. To Grant and Osborn, however, the war only heightened their concern because they were worried about the disproportionate number of Nordics being slaughtered in the trenches. Arguing that courage and a fighting spirit were distinctly Nordic traits, they feared that the best part of their gene pool was being destroyed. "War is in the highest sense dysgenic rather than eugenic," Osborn explained in a later edition of Grant's book. "It is destructive of the best strains, spiritually, morally, and physically."

In 1918, Osborn and Grant helped to form the Galton Society as an organization to study human anthropology, evolution, and eugenics. Anthropology was still a relatively new science, and they were worried that it was falling too much under the influence of Franz Boas (1858–1941), a Jewish American anthropologist at Columbia University. A somewhat short and balding man, Boas was unlike the eugenicists in that he believed in the equipotentiality of all people, and argued against what he called "this Nordic nonsense." In particular, Boas championed the idea that the environment played an outsized role in human society, contrary to the thinking of Galton, and he helped to usher in the so-called nature-versus-nurture debate, which challenged the idea that human potential was strictly a matter of one's genes. To Boas, genetics was just one part of an equation that also included the circumstances of one's environment and upbringing in determining a person's overall outcome in society.

Boas had for a long time been countering the eugenicists. In 1912, he had published a work called "Changes in Bodily Form of Descendants of Immigrants," in which he showed that the so-called cephalic index, or head size, data of children born in the United States differed from that of their immigrant parents, thus showing that living conditions could act to shape supposedly "immutable" racial traits. Eugenicists believed that such indices were determined purely by heredity, and Madison Grant was so threatened by any suggestion to the contrary that he wrote the president of the United States—William Howard Taft—to explain that "the structural differences between the main races of mankind are of immense antiquity," and that it was hardly credible that the physical characteristics of the "undesirable races" could be affected by environmental conditions in just one generation.

Resorting to personal attacks, Grant accounted for Boas's "silly" claims by pointing to the fact that he was Jewish, and that as a Jew he "represents a large body of Jewish immigrants, who resent the suggestion that they do not belong to the white race." Grant even went so far as to suggest that head size data for recent immigrants might possibly be the result of immigrant mothers having clandestine affairs with native-born Americans. Having once visited Poland himself, Grant despised "the wretched mass of degraded human beings" he saw there, living amidst "filth and unsanitary conditions." Referring to Jews, Grant claimed that they, "like rats, have formed a race able to survive gutter conditions which quickly destroy the higher types."

For his part, Boas held firm to his conviction that human ability was not determined so much by inheritance as the eugenicists supposed. He explained that there was more variation within each race than there was between them, and that a person's environment—the sum total of their living conditions—accounted for most of the racial distinctions that did exist. Grant and Osborn wanted to hear nothing of it. Instead, they redoubled their efforts to promote the Nordics. And one of the ways in which they did so was to turn to that quintessential Nordic in their midst—Roy Chapman Andrews.

In Andrews, eugenicists like Grant and Osborn found the perfect example of a White American. It was not just his good looks—firm jaw, light eyes—but also his disposition. He was intelligent and lion-hearted. In Andrews, Osborn saw the perfect embodiment of a Nordic, and he was eager to put him forward as the best example of his deeply held racial beliefs. *Under a Lucky Star* was the title of Andrews's autobiography, and indeed, opportunities seemed to fall right into his lap. But it was more than just luck, because Osborn had been promoting Andrews for years. Andrews would serve as the poster child to Osborn's pseudoscientific ideas, but on a more practical level, Osborn hoped that Andrews would be the man to one day deliver the proof for his assumption of the central Asian origins of man.

If Osborn could prove the central Asian origins of man, he believed it would prove the superior status of the Nordic race. Osborn expected to find a more generalized form of ancient human in central Asia. From this starting point, he hoped to then show how it evolved into new races as it invaded new territories. Osborn believed that the Nordics were the most highly advanced of all the races coming out of central Asia because of the fact that they evolved in the icy realm of northern Europe.

But more than just wanting to prove his own hypothesis, Osborn hoped to answer more practical questions about how civilization should be ordered. As far as Osborn was concerned, the Nordics were still evolving, and he pointed to the Nordics who had migrated across the Atlantic to North America as representing the highest state of their evolution. To Osborn, the most adventurous and daring of all the Nordics were the ones with the courage to settle in new lands, including those who had come to North America to forge what would become the United States of America.

Influenced by his evolutionary ideas, Osborn believed that human evolution was the story of progress, and that the ascent of the races of man was the result of a deliberate effort. "The moral principle inherent in evolution is that nothing can be gained in this world without an effort," he asserted, adding that "the ethical principle inherent in evolution is that only the best has the right to survive."

Osborn postulated that human evolution must have taken place in challenging environments, and theorized that modern humans must have first evolved on the high plains of northern Asia, and that they further improved themselves as they radiated outward and invaded still more challenging environments. He surmised that "the evolution of man is arrested or retrogressive in every region where the natural food supply is abundant and accessible without effort." He had made up his mind that humans could never have advanced in the tropics, and most especially not in Africa.

In the end, Osborn concluded that "while the anthropoid apes were luxuriating in the forested lowlands . . . the *Dawn Men* were evolving in the invigorating atmosphere of the relatively dry uplands." All Osborn needed now was the proof. He needed to find his *Dawn Man* in central Asia, and was resting all his hopes on Roy Chapman Andrews.

CHAPTER TWELVE

Monkey in the Middle

Carl Akeley came back from Africa a changed man. Having gone to kill elephants, he returned determined to champion the continent's fast-vanishing wildlife. His near-death experience had changed him. It was as if that elephant on Mt. Kenya was not trying to kill him so much as shake him into action, and even before the bandages were removed from his head, Akeley had formulated a vision for what he would call Africa Hall. As he described it, he wanted to create a space that would "tell the story of jungle peace; a story that is sincere and faithful to the African beasts as I have known them." What Akeley wished to create was a monument to Africa—a tribute to the continent and its wildlife.

Akeley presented his idea to Osborn in 1912, sketching out plans for a large gallery with a wraparound balcony encompassing no fewer than forty full-sized habitat dioramas. Each diorama would comprise a group of taxidermy animals against a panoramic landscape, and with elements of foliage in the foreground to exactly replicate a real place in Africa. As Akeley explained it, he would put the utmost care into making his dioramas so realistic that a visitor would have the illusion, at the very least, of "passing a series of pictures of primeval Africa." At best, Akeley hoped his dioramas would transport the viewer "five thousand miles across the sea into Africa itself."

Osborn loved the idea, as did the museum's trustees, who saw it as a means to "preserving forever" the majesty of Africa. Osborn thought it would be the start of "a great new era in nature education at the Museum." Having long pushed for programs designed to teach city schoolchildren about the morality inherent in nature, Osborn saw Africa Hall as fostering this same goal. "We have been searching for years for a means of teaching the lessons of nature to the people of the city," he later wrote, but "after African Hall was built, the Museum could take these people to Africa. The lessons of nature will thus be taught in this city." So encouraged was Osborn that he floated the idea of creating similarly themed halls for the mammals of North America and Asia, and predicted that "the building of the African Hall would put the American Museum first among all the natural history museums in the world."

As plans for Africa Hall moved forward, Carl and Delia adjusted to life in New York City, and moved into a spacious three-bedroom apartment just a few blocks from the museum on Central Park West. After years of living in the African bush, they could finally feel somewhat civilized—*somewhat*, because joining them in their sunny apartment was J. T. Jr., the little monkey that Delia insisted on bringing back from Africa. The simian was given her own room with treetop views of Central Park, assuring Delia that she would feel at home in her new urban jungle. Together, Carl and Delia lived with the monkey as if it were their child.

Akeley was eager to begin work on Africa Hall, but the museum was still looking for donors to sponsor the project. In the interim, Akeley worked out of James Clark's taxidermy studio in the Bronx, where he completed animals for the Field Museum and other clients. It was during this time that he also devised a motion picture camera specifically for use in the field. As Akeley put it, "there was no movie director to tell my untutored animal actors where to move in order to keep within the field of the camera lens, so they were apt to, very often, jump clear of the picture at the most interesting moment." Having had so much trouble with the clunky cameras on the market at that time, he began tinkering with the idea of a swivel-mounted camera. In just a few short months, Akeley had invented a new camera that was better than anything else on the market.

Yet Africa Hall remained Akeley's main goal, and he was eager to start work in earnest. Osborn assured him of his "undiminished interest" in the project, but rumors of war in Europe put a damper on its funding. Two years passed without much support, and by the summer of 1914, Akeley expressed his misgivings: "My seeming impatience is because I feel the urgency of getting the work started. . . . I do not intend to accept half-hearted support. I need enthusiastic support of the museum authorities to insure the doing of a big thing in a big way. I shall withdraw my proposals only when I am convinced that the apparent indifference is real and not caused by unfortunate conditions in the business world." Circulating copies of Akeley's letter among the trustees, Osborn implored them to move things along or risk losing the only man who could complete the job.

To keep interest in the project alive, Akeley worked on a scale model of *Africa Hall*. Full of little clay animals, it was the first concrete expression of his vision, and he rendered it in meticulous detail. Even in miniature form, his dioramas seemed to capture the feeling of Africa. The model sat on a table in his expansive studio on the second floor of the museum's east wing, and nearly every day prospective backers and trustees visited Akeley's studio to examine the model. Funds dribbled in slowly, and with the outbreak of war in the summer of 1914, all plans for Akeley to return to Africa were halted. Expeditions were suspended, and all Akeley could do was work on the elephants he had already collected years before.

Akeley took this downtime to further refine his elephant taxidermy techniques. It had been nearly thirty years since he first mounted Jumbo's skin for P. T. Barnum. Also, he had never really been happy with the methods he used to mount the fighting bulls at the Field Museum. Mounting the Chicago elephants involved building up a structural armature that was then filled out with wire mesh and a layer of plaster reinforced with tow fiber. Over this manikin were arranged large sections of the tanned elephant skin, each being secured with injections of gluey plaster administered through strategic slits in the skin that were later sealed up with beeswax. While this method proved to be satisfactory, Akeley was never quite happy with the relatively short period of time this method gave him to model all the textural details into the skin before the underlying layer of gluey plaster dried.

At the American Museum, Akeley had the idea of making a full-sized clay rendering of an elephant from which he then planned to mold and cast a full manikin, but he quickly realized that instead of attempting to mount the skin *over* some kind of prefabricated form, he might instead create a supporting structure little by little from *inside* the elephant. In this way, Akeley could better re-create all the folds and textures into the elephant's tanned skin first, fixing them in place with layers of plaster only after he was completely satisfied with the results.

Tanning the elephant hides was another matter, and Akeley had two assistants assigned to the task. Every day they hoisted the skins out of the enormous tanks of brine in which they soaked so that they could continue to pare down the fleshy side of the skin with small knives. Weeks of slicing ensued, until all four elephant skins were a uniform thickness of about a quarter inch. Next they were moved into a tanning bath, where they had to soak for a full three months while being turned and agitated frequently. Finally, after months of effort, the skins were rinsed and rubbed with oil until they were as fine and supple as leather gloves.

Meanwhile, Akeley worked on a scale model of his proposed elephant group. Reviewing all his notes, measurements, and photographs made in the field, he refined this scale model until he had worked out the exact poses he wanted for each of the four elephants. Only then did he begin the process of actually mounting the skins. He was a perfectionist, and so consumed with his art that he sometimes seemed oblivious to the world around him, at one point even arriving at the museum wearing mismatched shoes. One of his closest friends, Andrews, later told of how Akeley did not lead a balanced life. "He had no hours of play, as an ordinary man conceives it. The particular problem on which he was working at the moment seemed to occupy his mind so completely that he would relegate it to the subconscious background for only a short time," he wrote.

But something else was on Akeley's mind, even if he wanted to forget. His personal life was a train wreck. Rather than going home to Delia—who always seemed more interested in her monkey—Akeley spent long hours in his elephant studio. Delia may have been captivated by Carl as an erstwhile teenage runaway and young bride, but with Akeley devoting all his attentions to Africa Hall, she sometimes felt abandoned. For too long her own ambitions had been tied to her husband's, and she longed to find a purpose in life all her own.

For a time, Delia fancied herself an ethologist, taking it upon herself to study her pet monkey while attempting to document all the ways in which she adjusted to civilization. She doted on the monkey, and the animal started to demand all her attention. The monkey became enraged every time Delia tried to leave the apartment, at one point raiding her closet and destroying all her fancy clothes, while leaving the more mundane outfits she normally wore around the house intact. In desperation, Delia hung a leopard skin over her dresser, hoping that the monkey might still have a primal fear of the African predator's spots.

And then there was the smell, which at times was as awful as Akeley's taxidermy studio. It was all but impossible for the Akeleys to invite guests over. It wasn't long before Delia refused to leave the apartment, even for important museum events. She became completely obsessed with her monkey and sat around the apartment all day playing with the animal. One day, J. T. Jr. got upset after seeing a procession of circus elephants from her window overlooking the park. Delia had to cradle her in her arms and play soft music to get her to settle down. She seemed to care for little else, and became a slave to the captive animal, writing that she wished to do nothing more than devote herself to "the care and study of this interesting little creature."

After a time, Delia started to think that the animal could understand human language and that she could even answer with the single English word *yes*. The two grew so interdependent on each other that Akeley quite understandably grew jealous. Night after night, he lingered in his studio while his marriage imploded, even as his elephants slowly took on the appearance of life. Obsessed with making his elephants perfect, he stayed up late reviewing the motion pictures that he had taken of living elephants in order to more accurately capture their motion in his taxidermy.

At last, the little monkey grew so incorrigible she attacked Delia, biting her severely on the leg. The wound required surgery, which Delia insisted on having at home so that she would not have to leave her pet. As Delia hobbled around on her cane during her recovery, J. T. Jr. lashed out at her again, this time leaping on her from an elevated hiding space and going for her neck. Shortly thereafter, she attacked Delia yet again, nearly puncturing an artery and severing a nerve in her wrist.

Akeley had seen enough. He made arrangements for J. T. Jr. to go to the National Zoo in Washington. Delia did not protest, but after the monkey was gone she cried for days, feeling lost and empty. Having no other friends, she stayed home alone while Akeley went to his studio. Then one day Carl came home to find that Delia was gone. She had sold her trophy elephant tusks to the museum—the record tusks she had taken from Mt. Kenya on their honeymoon safari—and used the $1,500 to run off to France, following the American

Expeditionary Forces to the Western Front, where she volunteered in the field hospitals.

Akeley was infuriated, and waited bitterly all through the war for her return. When she failed to appear after the armistice, he thought that maybe something terrible had happened, until mutual friends let him know that indeed she had returned to New York and had already been living in the city for several months. She had even made the trip to Washington to visit her imprisoned monkey, but she did not bother to see her husband. Clearly their marriage was over, but it would be several more years before they officially divorced.

Akeley was now fifty-five years old, and although the museum was eager to get on with the work of *Africa Hall*, he was too deeply depressed to do much work. Osborn tried to convince donors that Akeley had resumed his work "with great vigor," but the truth was that Carl could not summon any enthusiasm. The elephants that he and his estranged wife had collected together on their honeymoon remained in a suspended state, just like his marriage.

At the same time, Akeley struggled to raise funds for his next African expeditions, in no small part because he was now in competition with Andrews for access to the same wealthy donors. Ideally, Akeley hoped to find a single wealthy donor—a great man to solve all his problems—but unlike Andrews, he was hardly as talented a fundraiser. He may have had an interesting life, but he was too moody and introspective to be much good at working up a donor. For a time he traveled the lecture circuit, telling of his tales in the jungle, yet his heart was never really in it. Without Delia, Carl had lost his muse.

Akeley slowly reverted to a bachelor's way of life. He started seeing other women, and on an impulse, he bought himself a new Buick. This gave him greater freedom to get out of the city, and soon afterward he was taking various women on long weekend trips to the country. Eventually he settled into an affair with a young female mountain climber and explorer named Mary Lenore Jobe, even though he was still technically married.

Through it all, Akeley was inactive in the studio, and Osborn became annoyed that his chief taxidermist seemed to have abandoned all his ambitions. A year passed, and then another, but still he was not done with his elephants. A full ten years had passed since he first shot the elephants, and still they were not done. Even as some building planners came to the museum to review Akeley's plans, they found that his *Africa Hall* model was in a dilapidated condition. Osborn blamed Akeley, who in turn complained that he received no assistance from the museum for even the carpentry work.

Osborn's new urgency to complete *Africa Hall* was related to his plan to move forward with a gigantic memorial to Theodore Roosevelt, who had died shortly after the end of the war. He wanted to build a grand rotunda to simultaneously serve as the museum's new entrance off Central Park as well as the gateway to Akeley's *Africa Hall.*

To Osborn, Roosevelt embodied the ideal man—a Nordic who exhibited all the requisite qualities of intelligence, courage, and high achievement. Roosevelt was the man Osborn thought everyone should strive to emulate, and Akeley was enamored with him, too, at one point even speaking admirably of Roosevelt to the point of professing love. It is not surprising, therefore, that they eventually decided to include *Africa Hall* as part of a much larger memorial to Roosevelt.

But Osborn wished to showcase more than just Africa and its vanishing wildlife. To him the hall was a symbol of the end of the "age of mammals" and the beginning of what he called the "age of man." Africa was the last place on Earth where one could still observe a thriving megafauna, complete with lions, rhinoceros, elephants, and vast herds of ungulates. But as a paleontologist, Osborn knew that a similar megafauna once roamed Europe and North America, too. Although known only from fossils, there used to be lions, and mastodons, and woolly rhinoceros throughout Europe and North America. They were all extirpated shortly after the end of the last

Ice Age—the victims of marauding *Dawn Men*—but they still hung on in Africa. To Osborn, the intact megafauna of Africa was proof of the superiority of the Nordic race, his twisted logic being that the native Africans alone were not capable of vanquishing their megafauna. For that, they needed the superior extermination skills of the Nordics, who had only just arrived on the continent as big-game hunters.

Theodore Roosevelt had lyrically described his passage through East Africa as "a railroad through the Pleistocene," believing the large mammals he was about to hunt would soon follow a path to extinction. And he mirrored Osborn's way of thinking by likening himself to a modern-day *Dawn Man* in his narrative of his Africa safari. Roosevelt describes how his experience "did not and does not differ materially from what it was in Europe in the late Pleistocene." He then went on to describe how this comparison was not fanciful: "The teeming multitudes of wild creatures, the stupendous size of some of them, the terrible nature of others, and the low culture of many of the savage tribes, especially of the hunting tribes, substantially reproduces the conditions of life in Europe as it was led by our ancestors ages before the dawn of anything that could be called civilization. The great beasts that now live in East Africa were in that bygone age represented by close kinsfolk in Europe and in many places up to the present moment. African man, absolutely naked, and armed as our early Paleolithic ancestors were armed, lives among, and on, and in constant dread of, these beasts, just as was true of the men to whom the cave-lion was a nightmare of terror, and the mammoth and the woolly rhinoceros possible but most formidable prey. The region, this great fragment out of the long-buried past of our race, is now accessible by railroad."

Unwilling to believe that man evolved in Africa, Osborn was liable to view its unusually rich and diverse megafauna as proof of his conjecture. As he would later explain, "Africa is the only continent which preserves entire the life of the earth before man entered it as the destroying angel. It is still a living picture of the 'great age of mammals,' to use the telling phrase of Louis Agassiz, as it existed in all its grandeur before the age of man."

According to Osborn, Africa still retained its rich megafauna precisely because the ancestors of his *Dawn Man*—the Nordics—had only just begun to penetrate the Dark Continent. To Osborn, Akeley's proposed *Africa Hall* was a validation of his human origins thesis. When completed, he believed, it would stand as a monument to the conquering power of the Nordics—"to the life of the Ancient World—a monument which twenty-five years hence, and even a less period, it will be impossible to erect." The whole point of *Africa Hall* was to "fix a reality for time to come, and to extend the actual experience of consciousness." The completed hall would stand as a constant reminder of the heights to which man had evolved, and a testament to the conquering power of the Nordics, who thanks to the railroads were just beginning their conquest of Africa.

Though grandiose in its conception, if *Africa Hall* was to become a reality, it depended on a frail and chronically depressed famous taxidermist motivating himself to work. Still in a funk and unable to muster much enthusiasm for his work, Akeley thought that perhaps a return to Africa might rekindle his former passions. More than anything, he wanted to collect some gorillas. The species had only been recently reported from the far eastern limits of the Belgian Congo, and that was enough to inspire Akeley to go. The year was 1921, and for the fourth time in his life, Akeley prepared to embark on another great African adventure.

CHAPTER THIRTEEN

New Conquest

Having crisscrossed the Far East as both an explorer and a spy, Roy Chapman Andrews could certainly tell some good stories. He had been abandoned on a deserted island off the coast of Borneo, hunted a man-eating tiger through the jungles of Burma, and survived gunfights with bandits in Mongolia. He was unquestionably a man of adventure, but as he matured into middle age, Andrews longed for something more than mere thrills. He wanted to contribute something to society, and as he returned to New York in 1920, he was thinking more and more about science.

A short while after stepping ashore, Andrews met Osborn at the American Museum for lunch. Entering the museum's second-floor dining hall, which overlooked the Seventy-Seventh Street entrance that he had so timidly entered as a new employee several years before, Andrews kept his poise as he sat down at the president's table. He had a bold new idea to present, but knowing how Osborn disliked discussing business over a meal, he tactfully waited until after coffee was served and they were both leisurely smoking. "Now let's have it, Roy," the boss finally said over a puff of smoke. "It's another expedition I suppose." Indeed it was, and with great earnestness Andrews detailed his plan for a new adventure in central Asia. Admitting that some of his previous expeditions were more like hunting trips, he presented a thoroughly scientific agenda to explore Mongolia and the Gobi Desert.

"We should try," he explained, "to construct the whole past history of the Central Asian plateau—its geology, fossils, climate, and vegetation. We've got to collect its living mammals, birds, fish, reptiles, insects, and plants, and map the unexplored parts of the Gobi." Volunteering himself as the leader of his proposed Central Asiatic Expedition, Andrews wished to survey the full spectrum of life—past and present—across all of Mongolia, and even into parts of China. Dreaming big, he even considered bringing along a motion picture crew to document the expedition. "It must be a thorough job; the biggest land expedition ever to leave the United States."

Years before, Osborn had issued his well-known "prophecy" that central Asia would be identified as an important center of origin for mammalian life, but he was never able to prove it. At that time, the earliest human was known from a fossil collected in Java. A Dutch explorer named Dubois had uncovered it in 1891—just a skull fragment, some teeth, and the head of a femur—but it was enough to establish the fossil as an upright walking hominoid. The so-called Java Man suggested that Asia, not Africa, was the cradle of humanity, but the proof was still inconclusive.

Osborn clung to the race-anxious notion that Whites, especially the so-called Nordics of northern Europe, had a separate origin from the peoples of Africa and elsewhere. The idea that a northern European race could trace its origins back to Africa, with its dark-skinned peoples, seemed only remotely possible to him. He had studied the distributions of mammals around the world, and to his mind, central Asia was the obvious biogeographic locus from which most mammals seemed to originate, including humans. He remained convinced that fossilized human ancestors would eventually be found there, but he still lacked proof.

The clash of dinnerware subsiding as their afternoon luncheon wore on, Osborn looked back at Andrews as he finished his pitch. Square jawed and squinty eyed, Andrews was a quintessential Nordic, and Osborn must have sensed a certain karma in him proving his race concept right. But Andrews's idea wasn't without its challenges. The expedition was as scientifically ambitious as it was daring, and Osborn worried about the logistics. The Gobi Desert was second in size only to the Sahara, and it spanned hundreds of desolate miles. How would the expedition cover such distances?

Andrews's solution was novel for the time—automobiles. Supported by a caravan of camels, they would first cache food and gasoline at set points along their planned route, and then they would use a fleet of motorcars to race across the desert. From his own experiences Andrews knew that Mongolia's gravel-covered landscape—dotted here and there with sand dunes and rocky outcrops—was essentially drivable. So long as he could keep the supply caravan intact, automobiles were the most effective way to survey the desert. As Andrews explained it, camels averaged only ten or fifteen miles a day, but automobiles could easily cover hundreds. "If all goes as expected," he continued, "we could do ten years' work in five months."

Still, Osborn had his doubts. Save for a single tooth of an extinct rhinoceros picked up along a caravan trail in 1894, nobody had ever reported a fossil from Mongolia. What's more, most scientists believed this tooth had been dropped by traders supplying China's apothecary shops and that it could have come from almost anywhere—why Mongolia? In response Andrews could only plead that previous explorers had never really looked for fossils in the region, and that he would be able to cover considerable ground. Glaring back at Osborn, Andrews went on to explain how prospecting for fossils by automobile had the potential to make history, if only he were given the chance. It was the most important sales pitch of his career, and Andrews kept his cool while delivering it. Nothing like what he was proposing had ever been attempted before. Osborn knew the expedition was a gamble, but looking back at Andrews, he could not help but give the man a chance.

Andrews estimated his Central Asiatic Expedition—really a series of smaller expeditions over the course of several years—would cost a quarter of a million dollars. This was far more than Osborn could commit from the museum's coffers. He could promise staff, and perhaps as much as five thousand dollars a year, but Andrews would have to raise all the rest. Pointing him to some of the museum's most reliable donors, Osborn was certain that with Andrews's unbridled ambition, the funds were all but assured.

J. P. Morgan was the first man on his list, and Andrews bet that if he could get him to contribute, others would feel socially pressured to follow. Meeting in the sumptuous Morgan Library, with its wood-paneled walls and frescoed ceiling, Andrews spread out a map of central Asia. "There is always something exciting about a map," he later wrote, having specifically chosen one that still had some blank areas marked "unexplored." Theatrically pointing to the map, Andrews detailed his plan to use long caravans of camels in concert with a fleet of speedy automobiles to explore the desert. As he spoke, Morgan's eyes began to glow with excitement. "It's a great plan," he exclaimed. "I'll gamble with you."

Morgan committed $50,000 toward the expedition, launching Andrews on a whirlwind fundraising tour that at one point saw him attending thirty-two consecutive dinner parties full of laughs and champagne. Weary of these formalities, Andrews longed for a simple meal of just "crackers and milk" in his kitchen at home. Most of the donations were modest—just a few thousand dollars each—but when John D. Rockefeller matched J. P. Morgan's gift with an additional $50,000, it turned the Central Asiatic Expedition into a reality.

As soon as the expedition was announced, newspapers latched onto the romantic idea of searching Mongolia for lost ancestors, *The New York Times* running a dramatic headline—"Scientists to

Seek Ape-Man's Bones." As Andrews later described it, "primitive man was what they wanted and anything else bored them exceedingly." Soon Andrews's endeavor was known as the Missing Link Expedition.

The public was riveted, and Andrews received letters from people across the country volunteering their services. They came from former soldiers looking for adventure, bored men wanting to jazz up their life, and countless teenage boys for whom Andrews had become a hero. There was a letter from someone offering his services as a barber and sharpshooter, and another from a butcher who was sure he could serve as Andrews's bodyguard. A waiter wrote that he would like "to serve your tables in the Gobi," adding that he already owned a tuxedo.

There were so many letters that Andrews had to have standard rejection cards printed in bulk. Many thousands of letters were received from women. "If no position of secretary is open, perhaps you could take me just as a woman friend," one wrote, adding that she could create a cozy home atmosphere for Andrews. "I am sending my photograph," she added, "but it is much better to see the original. How would Friday afternoon do for tea?"

In the end, Andrews was careful about choosing only well-experienced men of science for the first expedition. Among those picked was his longtime friend Walter Granger. A curator of paleontology at the American Museum, Granger would serve as chief paleontologist and second in command. A mustachioed man with a hearty laugh, his competence as a paleontologist would allow Andrews to focus on managing the overall movements of the expedition without getting bogged down in the intricacies of excavating fossils. Having Granger also permitted Andrews some free time to hunt big game and collect specimens for the museum's planned Hall of Asian Mammals. The two men complemented each other perfectly, with Andrews's flamboyant style standing in contrast to Granger's scientific objectivity. Also joining the expedition were geologists, topographers, a photographer, Mongol interpreters, a herpetologist who also studied fish, and cooks and camp assistants who in total numbered more than twenty-six men.

For the expedition's official photographer, Andrews had hoped to hire the famed cinematographers Martin and Osa Johnson, but they had already committed to working with Akeley in East Africa. Instead, Andrews hired a little-known photographer named J. B. Shackelford, who had previously worked for the Akeley Camera Company that Carl had formed to sell the movie camera he had invented. With its quick-focus lens and precision panning mechanism, the Akeley camera was custom designed for wildlife cinematography. It had also proven equally well suited for combat photography, and Shackelford brought his own Akeley camera to film the Central Asiatic Expedition in Mongolia.

Equipment lists included everything needed for six months of work in the desert—dehydrated fruits and vegetables, flour, sugar, coffee, tea, and powdered milk. Canned hams and bacon were included to add variety to the wild game Andrews planned to shoot. Cigars, cigarettes, and a supply of whiskey and brandy were also included for special occasions. Among all the guns, ammunition, animal traps, picks, and shovels required to do their work, Andrews also listed a phonograph and records as luxuries he simply could not live without. Most crucial of all was the choice of automobile, and after much consideration, Andrews chose two one-ton Fulton trucks and three Dodge touring cars with open tops.

In planning his expedition, Andrews was especially mindful of how the natives of Mongolia lived. The indigenous people of Mongolia had spent thousands of years adapting to the environment, learning through trial and error the best ways to survive. Adopting some of their methods, Andrews had sheepskin coats, trousers, and sleeping bags made, and ordered exact copies of the typical Mongolian tent—not the much bigger yurts, which were too heavy and impractical for frequent moves, but the more portable native Mongolian tent made from two layers of blue cotton held up by a single center pole. It was the ideal shelter for an expedition on the move, and it resisted wind and sandstorms better than anything available in European outfitting stores.

Finally, in February 1921, Andrews, Yvette, and their three-year-old son George left New York for China. After a year of unrelenting fundraising, interviews, lectures, and planning—and with thirty-eight tons of equipment and supplies—Roy Chapman Andrews was finally embarked. He arrived in Peking in April, and found the city enveloped in a yellow haze from an epic dust storm that stretched from the western deserts to more than sixty miles out to sea. For the Chinese, it was a bad omen—one that foreboded war, famine, and disease—but Andrews wasn't scheduled to go out into the field anytime soon. Having already planned his expeditions to unfold over the course of many years, his first order of business was settling into his new Peking headquarters, a former Manchu palace located just northeast of the Forbidden City.

Inside the walled compound, eight inner courtyards were surrounded by dozens of one-story houses, the largest of which was sumptuously furnished with ornately carved furniture, heavy damask curtains, and fine Oriental art to serve as the Andrews family residence. It was a palatial estate, but it lacked electricity or plumbing, so Andrews had it refurbished with five bathhouses, a garage for six cars, stables for horses, and a laboratory complete with a photography darkroom. Hiring a staff of cooks, launderers, gardeners, and maids, Andrews readied the compound for members of the expedition the following spring.

Andrews needed to get his supply caravan on its way months in advance, and through his local agents, he procured dozens of camels and experienced caravanners to lead them. Food, scientific equipment, and gasoline were all loaded in specially constructed wooden boxes, each camel carrying two on either flank. It being summer, the two-humped camels were shedding their long winter coats, and their plan was to use the shed fur—which could be pulled off in great swaths—for packing their fossils for return in these same supply boxes.

By April 1922—a full year after Andrews's own arrival—all the expedition members were assembled in Peking. From there they boarded a special train to the frontier city of Kalgan. Mongolia awaited them, and with their automobile engines roaring "like the prehistoric monsters" they had come to seek, they drove westward through the Great Wall to begin their expedition.

They followed the telegraph lines out of the city, and finding their first cache of gasoline crates intact at the designated telegraph station, they pressed on toward Urga. There, after two weeks of negotiations, they received permission to collect fossils in Mongolia. Their plan was to drive southwest across the grasslands of central Mongolia until they reached the Gobi Desert, where they planned to meet their supply caravan before venturing deeper into the desert toward the Altai Mountains. From there they would follow the mountain range east to a point where they hoped to intersect an old caravan trail that would take them full circle back north to Kalgan. Their circuit would traverse more than a thousand miles, with the expedition's members collecting fossils and other specimens at strategic points along the way.

Leading the expedition across the open grassland, Andrews soon encountered men who fled in terror at the sight of their automobiles. Jumping on their horses, they galloped off, leaving their women and children behind. Further accentuating the feeling of leaving the modern world behind was the realization that the wireless radio was not working. Aside from the rumors spread by passing caravans, the expedition would have no news from the outside world. Most disturbing of all were reports that the desert was full of bandits. One band in particular was supposed to number over a thousand brigands commanded by a well-known chief who supposedly enjoyed torturing and killing White men by skinning them alive.

As they traveled, the scenery changed from gently rolling hills to a rugged landscape of boulders and rocky outcrops. At last, they came within view of the village of Sain Noin Khan in a broad green valley. Andrews set up camp on a larch-forested hill overlooking the village, which he described as "an indescribably beautiful sight," with temple roofs, golden spires, and upturned gables glistening in "every color of the rainbow." At least that was his impression from a distance, but as he interacted with the villagers, he was appalled by their uncleanliness. "Every man and woman carried through life the bodily dirt which had accumulated since childhood, unless it is removed by some accident or years of wear."

Andrews was relieved to learn that his supply caravan was camped at a nearby hot spring, where the camels were being given a rest. The success of the entire expedition hinged on these seventy-five camels, led by a sinewy Mongolian named Merin. Andrews came to respect Merin as an incomparable "master of the desert." Yet Merin had only barely escaped the expedition's first clash with brigands. Several bands of would-be robbers had attacked their group, only to be driven off by rifle fire. One soldier assigned to protect the caravan boasted of having hit four or five of the brigands, who appeared to slump in their saddles as they galloped away, but the scientists took little comfort. Almost certainly, they felt, the bandits would continue to stalk the caravan.

More bad news came with the realization that there weren't any fossils in the hills around Sain Noin Khan. Indeed, the expedition hadn't found any fossils since leaving Urga, and Andrews was beginning to worry about the wisdom of staking his entire reputation on the expedition. They moved on through a wasteland of buttes and ravines until at last they penetrated the Gobi proper. "Desolate it is," Andrews remarked in his journal, "but undeniably beautiful and intensely interesting as deserts almost always are."

They entered the Gobi in the midst of a violent storm, sweaty and sunburned, and although the middle of summer, the temperature dropped to freezing as wind gusts blasted them with hail and snow in their open-air cars. When the storm cleared, they went out looking for a guide and found their best prospect in an impoverished man whose sole worldly possessions, Andrews noted, were "one wife, one horse, one sheep and one goat." Dressed in tatters, the nomad was nonetheless familiar with the desert, and he climbed into one of their cars puffing on a cigar that had been given to him. Beaming with delight, he led them southward into the Gobi until they saw the jagged outline of the Altai Mountains on the horizon.

They made their camp beside an ancient well on a ridge above some gullies, where they found fossils in abundance. By the evening of their second day, they had filled several canvas bags with fossils—mammals, delicately preserved fish, plants, and insects in thin slabs of shale. Paleontologists rarely dig for fossils; rather, they scour the ground and rocky outcrops for little bits of bone embedded in surrounding rock, or matrix, as it is called. Although plenty of bones littered the ground beneath their feet, these were just the crumbs of skeletons that had long since weathered out of the rock. What the paleontologists were on the lookout for were intact fossil skeletons that were just beginning to erode from the surrounding matrix. Using delicate picks and brushes, they would then carefully clear away the matrix until they had partially revealed their prize. These they would carefully protect by painting them with gum arabic adhesive, reinforced with strips of rice paper and finally a "jacket" of flour-based plaster. As a last step, the entire jacketed fossil would be carefully pried from the ground so that it could be shipped back to the museum, where it would be opened and more carefully picked clean in a laboratory environment.

Andrews was too impatient for such work, and so he left the paleontologists to go about their business while he went off hunting big game with his rifle. The prospects for good hunting were perhaps the reason why the expedition next moved to what was called their Wild Ass Camp. Known only from the more arid parts of northeast Africa and central Asia, the primitive horses were of interest to Andrews, who was soon chasing after them in his motorcar at forty-five miles an hour. He was trying to clock their top speed, and Shackelford kept his Akeley camera on them along the way. Andrews chased one for twenty-nine miles before it dropped from exhaustion. In the end, they killed more than twenty stallions, mares, and colts for the museum. A mammalogist by training, Andrews also set traps for the smallest of species, and collected hundreds of mice, hedgehogs, and a kind of hopping rodent called a jerboa, which later proved to be a new species that was named after him–*Stylodipus andrewsi.* All these animals were processed by their Chinese taxidermists, and their preserved skins and skulls were later added to the collections of the American Museum, where they remain today.

Meanwhile, Granger kept busy uncovering the well-preserved bones of Cretaceous dinosaurs, among them a magnificent creature with a parrot-like beak that was later classified by Osborn as *Psittacosaurus mongoliensis.* Larger than this dinosaur was the colossal skull of a rhino-like Oligocene animal called an *Indricotherium.* Long touted as the largest land mammal that ever lived–far larger than any elephant–it stood more than fifteen feet tall at the shoulder and had a body length of more than twenty feet. Weighing an estimated thirty tons, its skull alone measured almost five feet long.

The expedition may have procured an abundance of fossils, but there were still no ancient humans among them. Andrews moved their camp to the shores of a glistening lake twenty miles to the southwest. Roughly three miles long and two miles wide, Tsagan Nor, or White Lake, teemed with water birds and small fish. Andrews declared it "exceptionally well suited to our purposes," and almost without break, they were kept busy with its rich fauna. They remained at White Lake until the middle of August, when they noticed a distinct chill in the air. Worried about the onset of the Mongolian winter, Andrews pressed on toward the eastern end of the Altai Mountains.

"The persistent chill," Andrews wrote, "was a warning to put the long stretch of unknown desert behind us without delay." Snow was falling on the distant mountains, forcing Andrews to announce that nothing except the discovery of the "missing link" would keep them in the field past September. Heading east, they got lost on the almost featureless land, and spent three days in a futile search for a route northward to Kalgan. Andrews had expected to encounter nomads to guide them, but they traveled nearly a hundred miles before they finally came upon a cluster of yurts.

Leaving Shackelford to wait in the other car, Andrews conferred with the Mongols, when a most fortuitous thing happened. While waiting for Andrews, Shackelford wandered away to inspect an unusual-looking outcrop. After walking a few yards, he found himself looking into a sweeping basin filled with spectacular formations cut by erosion into massive walls of reddish-orange sandstone. "Almost as if led by an invisible hand," Andrews later recounted, Shackelford had "walked straight to a small pinnacle of rock on top of which rested a white fossil bone. Below it the soft sandstone had weathered away, leaving it balanced and ready to be plucked off." It was later identified as some kind of reptile skull, but more important to them was their discovery of the fossil beds themselves. Everyone spent the remaining daylight hours scouring the area. The ground was littered with bones, with many more still eroding out of the rock all around them.

"It was one of the most picturesque spots that I have ever seen," said Andrews. "From our tents, we looked down into a vast pink basin, studded with giant buttes like orange beasts, carved from sandstone there appear to be medieval castles with spires and turrets brick-red in the evening light, colossal gateways, walls and ramparts. Caverns run deep into the rock and a labyrinth of ravines and gorges studded with fossil bones make it a paradise for paleontologists." Andrews would name this place the Flaming Cliffs on account of its brilliant red and orange colors, but he could hardly then suspect that it would become one of the most important fossil deposits in all of Asia.

Eventually the explorers were reunited with their caravan. Snow flurries fell in a chilly wind as they left Mongolia, and on the afternoon of September 18—and with their Klaxon horns blaring to announce their return—the expedition passed back through Kalgan's gates. After five months in the field, the first of Roy Chapman Andrews's Central Asiatic Expeditions was a success. He was sure that it would only be a matter of time before he found his much-sought-after missing link.

CHAPTER FOURTEEN

Murder on the Mountain

Doctor Savage—a Christian missionary first, and physician only when necessary—had spent more than a decade evangelizing in Liberia, the West African nation of freed American slaves. He had saved many African souls, he was sure, but at the cost of his own first two wives, both of whom died of tropical fever. Now with his own health failing, Savage was finally going home. America awaited him, but not long after the start of his journey, his ship was unexpectedly detained at the mouth of the Gabon River. It was 1846, and the doctor would remain in sultry equatorial Africa for another month. Fortunately, he had the acquaintance of some fellow missionaries—the Reverend and Mrs. John L. Wilson—who welcomed the traveler into their riverside home.

Like Savage, the Wilsons had lived in Africa a long time, and the interior of their bamboo-slat home was filled with all kinds of African curiosities. Savage had seen the likes of much of it before, but one object in particular caught the doctor's eye. It was a skull, and vaguely reminiscent of a man. Staring deep into its hollow eye sockets, and examining its nearly two-inch-long fangs, Savage was convinced it belonged to a hitherto unknown species. It was some kind of *Orang*, as it were, but quite large, and with a rather slanted face and heavy brow. Local hunters told him the skull belonged to the *njena*, a kind of "monkey-like animal," of remarkable size and ferocity. It lived in the deepest jungle, they said, and what little they knew of these "wild men of the woods" passed from their lips to Savage's ear. The ailing doctor was certain the animal was something new, and as his ship finally set sail, he carried the skull home.

By the time he arrived back in the United States, Savage was "quite unwell." Unable to think very clearly, he passed the skull to his friend the Harvard anatomist Jeffries Wyman, who instantly recognized it as something new. Together Wyman and Savage described the fearsome animal as a new species in the December 1847 issue of the *Boston Journal of Natural History.* "This animal [is] much larger and more ferocious than the Chimpanzee," Wyman wrote. "They live in herds, the females exceeding the males in number," he continued, adding that the killing of one was deemed "an act of great skill and courage." He went on to describe how the animal's head was "longer than that of an ordinary man by two inches," but that its intelligence was "inferior to that of the Chimpanzee." Savage and Wyman both believed their new species was the closest living relative to humans, and in their formal description, they gave it the name we know it by today—the gorilla.

What we would today call the western lowland gorilla was certainly known to the Africans who coexisted with them in the remote interior. They had lived with the njena for millennia, but there were only scant accounts of sightings in the annals of Western scientific literature. Wyman and Savage's animal was just the first of two gorilla species, and four subspecies, that would eventually be recognized by scientists in the ensuing decades, but at the time of its first formal description, the true nature of the gorilla was something of a mystery. Scientists knew little about its life in the wild.

A more widespread awareness of the existence of the gorilla came only after the Franco-American explorer Paul Du Chaillu wrote about hunting them in the wild. The son of a French trader, Du Chaillu had followed his father to the colony of Gabon as a teenager. There he lived under the care of the ever-hospitable Reverend Wilson, whom he admired and respected more than his own oft-absent father. Listening to Wilson's stories of the mysterious gorilla nurtured Du Chaillu's appreciation for nature, and it was Wilson who later sent him to America, where he began to express himself in writing.

Standing just over five feet tall, with a wiry build and thick mustache, Du Chaillu was a compulsive raconteur. He was full of stories, and having written several popular articles on Africa for the *New York Tribune*, he attracted the attention of John Cassin, the head of the Philadelphia Academy of Natural Sciences. As a classic "armchair naturalist," Cassin rarely went afield himself, but rather practiced ornithology as a gentlemanly diversion. He sponsored a small army of bird collectors to outposts around the world, and recruited Du Chaillu to collect West African birds for the Philadelphia Academy. Led to believe that he would receive generous remuneration for his efforts, the young adventurer penetrated deep into the jungle by dugout canoe. Everyone thought he was crazy, but Du Chaillu had gone into the interior as a trader before. Choosing the Muni River, he endeavored to follow it upstream to the Crystal Mountains. Shooting and stuffing birds along the way, his secret goal was to come back with more than just pretty birds, for unbeknownst to anyone else, he was intent on getting gorillas.

Du Chaillu spent years exploring the jungle, assisted by men from the local tribes, and he sent thousands of bird specimens back to Philadelphia. All the while, he grew ever more determined as the natives told him stories of gorillas being possessed by the spirits of the dead, and of how they abducted women, and sometimes beat elephants to death with clubs. When he finally got his first glimpse of a living gorilla, the beast announced itself with a terrifying roar. It rose on two legs and charged. Du Chaillu stood by and watched as one of his men shot the beast dead at close range. It was a big male silverback, the first of many they would encounter. By the time Du Chaillu returned to America in 1859, he carried the preserved remains of more than twenty gorillas. His specimens ranged from big male silverbacks, to females and their suckling offspring, several of which he had tried to keep alive as captives. Killing these animals made him uneasy, if only because they seemed so human. "Though there are sufficient points of diversity between this animal and man," he wrote, "I never kill one without having a sickening realization of the horrid human likeness of the beast."

Du Chaillu may have been the first White man to tell of his adventures hunting gorillas in their natural habitat, but he was hardly welcomed back to the Philadelphia Academy. To the contrary, in his long absence, the members of that august body had shunned him. Nobody wanted to speak to him because they had come to suspect that he was the product of his father's dalliance with a mixed-race slave. Du Chaillu had tainted blood. He was an octoroon. They refused to pay him the $866.50 he claimed he was owed, and could not care less that he had collected the rare and elusive gorilla. The Philadelphia Academy wanted nothing to do with Paul Du Chaillu.

Frustrated, Du Chaillu abandoned science and tried to support himself in New York as an impresario. Rooming at the Five Points Mission, in the city's most infamous slum, he opened a modest exhibition hall on Broadway, just below Bleecker Street. Inside the long and narrow showroom, Du Chaillu displayed his large collection of African artifacts—several crates full of stuffed birds and spears and shields from various tribes. He hung hundreds of items up on the walls, but most impressive of all were the fourteen stuffed gorillas in the middle of the room, arranged in various threatening poses.

Eager to increase his profits, Du Chaillu made himself one of the attractions, telling stories of his harrowing experiences among the gorillas. Depicting gorillas as hairy man-devils of the forest, he described how a gorilla could seize a man's rifle and snap it in half. At the same time, he plugged the idea that they were much more closely related to humans than they actually were.

For a short time, things seemed to be going well for Du Chaillu. He had one-of-a-kind collections and a prime location on Broadway in which to show them. Unfortunately, the storefront was not all that far from where P. T. Barnum had his American Museum, and in 1860, the showman saw Du Chaillu as a threat. Having no hope of ever matching Du Chaillu's gorillas, Barnum resorted to an outright fabrication when he invented his *What is It?* Claimed to have been captured in the remote interior of Africa, Barnum's "nondescript" was in reality a Black man with microcephaly dressed up in an ape suit, but Barnum described him as nothing less than the "Connecting link between Man and Brute!!!!"

Not to be outdone, Du Chaillu decided to write a book about his experiences hunting gorillas—*Explorations and Adventures in Equatorial Africa*—and under the influence of his editors, his stories became tales of horrifying encounters between man and beast. Thus, the Western world's first impressions of the gorilla were deeply entwined with ugly racial stereotypes and the myth of their capacity for extreme violence.

Half a century later, in 1921, as Carl Akeley prepared to embark on his fourth trip to Africa, he struggled to pin down his own feelings about gorillas. Western perceptions of the great apes had hardly changed much since the days of Savage, Du Chaillu, and Barnum, and Akeley was not sure what to believe. It had been three-quarters of a century since Wyman and Savage first described the species, yet very little was known about the behavior of gorillas in the wild. Just thinking about gorillas made Akeley nervous and anxious, and he went back and forth in his mind trying to decide whether they were harmless or ferocious.

The first living gorilla that Akeley ever saw was a very young animal in the Zoological Park of London, and he was impressed by how it seemed to want nothing more than to be loved. "They appear to have an extremely affectionate disposition," he said of the captive. As for their kin living in the jungle, Akeley had spent enough time in Africa to know that animals rarely went looking for a fight. "The more I have seen of wild animals in Africa the less I have believed in their ferocity," he wrote. Still, he wasn't sure when it came to the gorilla. Something about the gorilla's human-like qualities made Akeley wonder if perhaps they might be capable of great violence. After all, the First World War had only just ended, so the idea of anthropoid apes committing extreme violence against one another was hardly far-fetched.

More than anything, Akeley wanted to be the first to film live gorillas in the wild, but his rifle was never far behind. "I hope that I shall have the courage to allow an apparently charging gorilla come within reasonable distance before shooting." Although hesitating to say just what he considered a reasonable distance, he added that "I shall feel very gratified if I can get a photograph at twenty feet. I should be proud of my nerve if I were able to show a photograph of him at ten feet, but I do not expect to do this unless I am at the moment a victim of suicidal mania." There being so much misinformation about gorillas, Akeley saw fit to write what became known as his "gorilla creed." Putting his thoughts down on paper was Akeley's way of mentally preparing himself for his first wild gorilla encounter:

"I believe that the gorilla is normally a perfectly amiable and decent creature. I believe that if he attacks man it is because he is being attacked or thinks that he is being attacked. I believe that he will fight in self-defense and probably in defense of his family; that he will keep away from a fight until he is frightened or driven into it. I believe that, although the old male advances when a hunter is approaching a family of gorillas, he will not close in, if the man involved has the courage to stand firm. In other words, his advance will turn out to be what is usually called a bluff. I believe, however, that the white man who will allow a gorilla to get within ten feet of him without shooting is a plain darn fool, for certainly the average man would have little show in the clutch of a three or four hundred pound gorilla."

To Akeley, the gorilla also seemed almost human, and he feared that he might find the act of killing one akin to murder. Would he be able to kill a gorilla? And would the act forever change how he felt about himself? Akeley was unsure, and his gorilla creed reads as both affirmation and confession. By his own account, Akeley set down his gorilla creed "for the purpose of recording the frame of mind with which I am going into the Kivu country to study, photograph and collect gorillas." Yet the undeniably human-like qualities of the gorilla continued to haunt him, and Akeley concluded his gorilla creed with a most disturbing addendum: "I look forward to the killing of these animals with as little pleasure as though I were going out to kill African natives. Of course, I realize that many people consider the shooting of [natives] as great sport. These same people would undoubtedly enjoy killing gorillas. During the coming months my opinions may suffer many changes."

To pay for his gorilla expedition, Akeley agreed to write a series of articles for *World's Work* magazine, and to give paid lectures upon his return. He would also escort a wealthy couple—Mr. and Mrs. Herbert Bradley—through southern Africa on a weeks-long shooting holiday. Accompanying them to Cape Town was the Bradleys' five-year-old daughter, Alice, and her nanny, Priscilla Hall. And Akeley himself had invited along Martha Miller, the niece of a family friend. The inclusion of women and a child on the expedition bemused Akeley. "I cannot possibly come back from this expedition as a hero because I am taking ladies and a little baby into a country that is full of beauty and charm, and I shall not be able to tell a tale of hardships and dangers overcome; but it is just as much fun to pull down the pedestals of fake heroes as it is to build the pedestal for yourself."

More than anything, Akeley went to Africa to "bring back stories of beautiful Africa, not of that horrible darkest Africa which the public has accepted." To Akeley, going after the gorilla was far more interesting than hunting lion or elephant simply because the animal was so poorly known. Not many people had studied gorillas in their native habitat, and it was considered to be one of the most remarkable animals in the world, "and when is added to that the fact that he is the nearest to man of any other member of the animal kingdom, a gorilla expedition acquires a tremendous fascination," Akeley remarked. Almost everything Akeley knew about gorillas came from his readings of Du Chaillu's hunting accounts, and he admitted to being fascinated with his stories. Du Chaillu had established the gorilla as "among the most powerful and ferocious animals on earth," and this reputation was so firmly established in the popular mind that Akeley's plan of taking ladies with no previous hunting experience of any kind into gorilla territory was "looked upon as madness."

But first, Akeley had to suffer through the holiday tour portion of his expedition. For six long weeks Akeley led the party north from Cape Town, traversing more than two thousand miles of terrain, most of it by train or boat, and Akeley remarked that they did not see "a single head of game," it having been so rapidly depleted along the major routes of transportation. This first part of the expedition made Akeley irritable, if only because it left him feeling as though no real work was being accomplished, and that it was all "a terrible loss of time." He was so anxious to get to the gorillas, Akeley admitted, that he was "not a very pleasant camp companion."

Finally, nearing the end of 1921, Akeley reached the northern shores of Lake Kivu at the eastern border of the Belgian Congo, and he wrote of how this "quickened the blood." He began to encounter certain traveling Belgian officials who told him stories of gorillas that had become so aggressive, they entered villages and drove out the natives. Again, Akeley was not quite sure what to believe, but decided that it was perhaps best for the women and children to stay behind in the village of Kisenyi while he and Mr. Bradley pushed farther into the Congo for gorillas.

It was a three-day walk from Kisenyi to the foot of Mt. Mikeno—one of the three Virunga volcanoes along the rift valley on the Congo frontier. This was the same place from which the Prince of Sweden had recently shot fourteen gorillas. Outfitted with some local guides,

Akeley was led up the side of Mt. Mikeno for two hours before he saw his first signs of gorillas. There was a little muddy spot, and in it was the unmistakable knuckle print of a gorilla. "I'll never forget it. In that mud hole were the marks of four great knuckles where the gorilla had placed his hand on the ground." Then Akeley started to doubt himself. "As I looked at that track I lost the faith on which I had brought my party to Africa. Instinctively I took my gun from the gun boy." Half an hour later he came upon more signs, "tracks made by the feet of the beast, enormous human-looking tracks showing the marks of a heel which no other living thing in the world but the gorilla and man has. I gave the boy back the Springfield and took the big .475 elephant gun. And although the next bit of going was hard and wearing, I carried the gun myself and trusted it to no gun boy."

But they only went so far before his guides wanted to turn back. "I offered the guides a king's ransom (in their eyes) if they would show me the old boy before dark." But they were "lackadaisical about the whole affair," and with the onset of the steady afternoon rains, they all decided it was time to head back to camp. None of his guides were at all interested in seeking gorillas, and Akeley decided that they were "entirely useless" for his purposes, so he walked on for an additional two and a half hours before he returned to his camp just at dusk.

The next morning, Akeley walked three hours to the village of a local chief who went by the name "sultan of Burunga," where he found a group of more willing natives. "There was a gleam of real hope," Akeley wrote, and he camped at Burunga for the night in the hopes of making a fresh ascent in the morning. His tent set up in "a wonderful spot" with views of the volcanoes Mikeno and Karisimbi just behind him, Akeley turned to look at the "rosy glow" of the active volcano Nyamulagira from his cot. In the morning, he would ascend the slopes straddling Mts. Mikeno and Karisimbi.

Akeley rose early the next morning. His guides told him to leave everything behind, including his camera and dissection kit, because they would be moving through very dense jungle on steep terrain. "It was up to them," Akeley concluded. "I had put myself in their hands. I wanted to at least see a gorilla. I still doubted that there could be such a thing in this part of the world—even though I had seen its tracks."

Sure enough, the climb was grueling, the terrain covered with such thick vegetation that they had to cut their way through it. Akeley slipped and skidded along the muddy slopes, his skin besieged by stinging nettles and biting ants. One of the guides, a young boy of about fourteen, heard a sound coming from across a ravine and pointed to some movement. "We watched closely for five minutes, then a great black head slowly appeared above the green—rather indistinct, but no doubt as to what it was." It was Akeley's first glimpse of a wild gorilla, and it left an "everlasting impression" totally different from anything he had expected. "In a solid wall of vivid green a great scraggly black head slowly rising into view where it remained motionless for perhaps a half minute." They were too far away to shoot, but Akeley was thrilled just to have had his first encounter with a wild gorilla.

They crossed the chasm and climbed up the other slope, making their way to a spot just below where they had seen the animals. Akeley had to constantly stop to catch his breath. Having climbed to a ridge more than one thousand feet above their camp, they suddenly heard a deep roar sounding from just above. Akeley readied himself as best he could. The terrain was so steep that he was in constant danger of slipping and falling into the chasm below. He feared that the recoil from his rifle might send him tumbling down. Finding a four-inch-thick sapling, he propped himself up against it just as he heard another roar from above. Then came a violent rush, and raising his rifle Akeley saw nothing but the swaying of vegetation. Then the dark mass of a gorilla's head appeared, and it roared one last time as Akeley fired his elephant gun. The body of a great silverback male came tumbling down the mountain slope, its four-hundred-pound mass gaining momentum all the way until it was stopped, not more than eight feet from where Akeley stood, by an overhanging tree on the brink of the three-hundred-foot-deep canyon below them. Akeley had killed his first gorilla.

Akeley made his way down the slope to where the dead gorilla lay, but because he was told to leave his tools in camp, he had nothing but a pocket knife on him with which to skin the animal. One of the guides assisted him with his own iron knife, as the others held onto the gorilla to keep it from falling down into the canyon. Getting the gorilla's skin and bones back to camp, Akeley spent the next two days carefully paring off bits of flesh from the hide, taking measurements and photographs, and making plaster casts of its face, hands, and feet.

At dawn the next morning, Akeley went back up to where he shot the silverback. Little did Akeley know that the day's events would prove a turning point in his life. They worked their way down several ridges, always cutting their own trail through the tangles of vegetation, when they came upon the trail of a band of gorillas. They followed this trail for about an hour when, suddenly, they heard a rock tumble down into the chasm. Soon they had caught up to the band, and Akeley missed a shot at another big silverback.

The shot set up a hysterical frenzy among the animals and they beat a hasty retreat as Akeley moved in after them. Once again, the hunters found themselves advancing with the care of mountain goats as they inched closer along the steep slopes of a canyon that plunged one hundred feet below. Akeley wedged himself into a bush so that the kick of the rifle would not send him tumbling down. An old female was only fifty feet above him. Akeley shot and was surprised when she came tumbling right down the slope straight toward him. He lost his balance in the frantic moments that ensued, and thought that her body would smack right into him and take them both down to their deaths in the ravine below. He ducked just as she tumbled over him, knocking him on the head in the process. As he started to get up, a squealing screaming ball of black fur rolled past him, touching him, and then two more—an "avalanche of gorillas"—raced after the female. Akeley thought that it was a charge but soon realized that the "others had followed her not in anger but in fear and because they accepted her lead without realizing that it was involuntary." The black ball of fur was the female's four-year-old son, following his mother in her roll down the mountain.

Akeley recovered his senses enough to pursue the youngster only to find him in a clearing, racing about terrified. One of the Africans speared the young gorilla as Akeley approached, but he was still alive as Akeley looked into his face. Akeley wrote: "There was a heart-breaking expression of piteous pleading on his face. He would have come into my arms for comfort." In that moment, as Akeley gazed into the dying youngster's eyes, something happened to him. Here he stood, locked in a moment of profound contact with a living gorilla, and what he saw in the youngster's eyes were emotions of terror and pain—familiar emotions registered in familiar ways. In that face he saw kinship, intelligence, and sensitivity. Akeley had a growing sense of being the "savage," the "aggressor," and the "murderer."

CHAPTER FIFTEEN

The Age of Man

While Carl Akeley was feeling like a murderer for killing the gorillas he needed for his Africa Hall, Henry Fairfield Osborn was rushing to finish an exhibition all his own. Begun in 1915, the Hall of the Age of Man was supposed to complement the museum's fourth-floor fossil halls—already chockablock with dinosaurs and fossil mammals—by depicting man's relationship to nature. Humans were the focus of the nascent hall, and in it Osborn saw an opportunity to present his own ideas on the origins of man.

In particular, Osborn wished to portray ancient man in the context of the Ice Age, and he began by commissioning Charles Knight to paint giant murals depicting the four seasons of the Pleistocene on every wall. Against this backdrop, Osborn drew analogies from his lifetime of studying fossil mammals, beginning with prehistoric horses. Automobiles had only just supplanted horses as the primary means of transportation in the 1920s, so they were familiar animals that evoked nostalgia for a more traditional way of life. They were also abundant in the fossil record, and Osborn had been studying them since his Princeton days.

Shown three dimensionally on the museum's fourth floor were the articulated skeletons of seven fossil horses, each representing what

Osborn interpreted to be a distinct stage in their evolution through geological time. From the diminutive *Eohippus* of the Eocene, through the three-toed *Mesohippus* of the Oligocene, and finally to the one-toed *Equus* of today, the lineup depicted the gradual development of adaptations for swift running, such as a reduction in the number of toes and an increase in overall size. As if marching through geological time, Osborn presented the evolution of horses as a gradual, linear progression toward the predetermined goal of greater speed.

Also shown in the hall were the skeletons of several different "races" of horses. Expertly mounted by the osteologist S. Harmsted Chubb, they ranged from the diminutive Shetland pony to the great Percheron draft horse. There was the lithe skeleton of the famous Arabian racehorse, Sysonby, in mid-gallop, and also a tableau of a rearing horse skeleton being subdued by an equally dynamic human man skeleton. The former was a dramatic representation that was meant to suggest how a single species could include a variety of races, while the latter highlighted "the dominion of man over this powerful animal through superior intelligence."

The extinct titanotheres—odd-toed herbivores closely related to rhinoceros—offered another object lesson in evolution. These large animals had a horn that grew from the front of the snout like a rhinoceros's. From the small nodules seen in the earliest fossils of the Eocene, to the outlandishly large and grandiose horns of later epochs, Osborn used these examples to warn of the dangers of "over-specialization," and of how the most extreme examples of evolution were not always beneficial. "A race of animals may expend its energy largely in the development of certain single organs, such as horns or tusks," Osborn explained, while pointing out that this would interfere with the proper development of the animal as a whole. Extreme specialization could lead to extinction, according to Osborn, and he held firm to his belief in the "law of the unspecialized," which favored those organisms that were—like his beloved Nordics—of a more generalized form.

To Osborn, the laws of evolution and extinction were more than just scientifically interesting. He believed that species evolved toward set goals, and that their racial distinctions were a reflection of adaptations to their particular environments. It was a belief system that made it all too easy for him to suggest that the various races of man should best stay put in the geographic parts of the world where they first evolved.

In every way, Osborn set out to make the new Hall of the Age of Man a three-dimensional expression of Men of the Old Stone Age, his magnum opus on human evolution. Casts of human fossils and their artifacts were arranged to present his view that all the races of mankind were separate species. Making this point abundantly clear were the racial busts by J. Howard McGregor, a Columbia University professor and zoologist with an artistic flair for sculpture. Assisted by Osborn, he reconstructed the three-dimensional visages of Neanderthal and other ancient hominid skulls alongside those of modern humans, which were invariably shown in a racial hierarchy with the white Nordics at the top.

Osborn held a triumphalist view of human evolution, and the Ice Age became his focus because he believed this was the proving ground of human evolution. Osborn wished to showcase the Ice Age context in which the Nordics evolved, but lacking sufficient evidence in the human fossil record, Osborn instead decided to make his point in a most unusual way—by using elephants.

Osborn had been studying the elephant family since his earliest days at the museum, and nearly half the Hall of the Age of Man was devoted to displaying several complete mounted skeletons of mastodons and mammoths. The hall featured the whole evolutionary history of elephants because Osborn thought their evolutionary history was directly analogous to that of humans. As Osborn explained it, "it has been deemed wise" to include in the hall "the entire history of the evolution of the proboscideans, which taken altogether is the most majestic line of evolution that has thus far been discovered."

Osborn explained his fascination with elephants further: "An insatiable Wanderlust has always possessed the souls of elephants as it has the tribes and races of man. . . . The romances of elephant migration and conquest are second only to the romances of human migration and conquest." Osborn believed that elephants were the best and most dramatic examples of how evolution worked.

The Hall of the Age of Man was the culmination of Osborn's efforts to make the American Museum a concrete expression of his scientific and social beliefs. Ever since the 1890s, the museum had conveyed preservationist concerns in its exhibits, and now Osborn sought to extend these themes beyond endangered animals and habitats to include the preservation of traditional social values, too. He was eager to finish the hall before the upcoming International Eugenics Congress, which Osborn agreed to host at the museum in 1921.

The Eugenics Congress was largely the brainchild of Madison Grant, whose book *The Passing of the Great Race* had become immensely popular with the resumption of large-scale immigration after the war. Grant's book was seen as a particularly important work among the eugenicists, and although Osborn confided to some of his fellow curators that he was troubled by the book's strident tone, he nonetheless endorsed it.

The International Eugenics Congress formally opened on September 22, 1921, with more than three hundred in attendance. At that time, eugenics was still considered a legitimate science, and as Madison Grant's biographer explains, the congress was "not a gathering of cranks." Osborn delivered the opening address, during which he stated that he hoped that Congress would foster support for permanent immigration restriction, stressing a need to prevent "the multiplication of worthless members of society." It was a sentiment that would lead, ultimately, to the passage of the Immigration Act of 1924, which severely limited immigration from all but the countries of northwest Europe, and completely banned immigrants from all of Asia.

Newspaper articles of the time informed readers that the delegates were extremely concerned about the future of the human race because of the threat of "race degeneration," and that most of the researchers had endorsed "strict laws rejecting the unfit immigrant as a necessity for the healthy racial progress of the American people." Two days later, a headline in *The New York Times* was explicit: "Eugenists Dread Tainted Aliens. Believe Immigration Restriction Essential to Prevent Deterioration of Race Here. Melting Pot False Theory. Racial Mixture Liable to Lower the Quality of the Stock—Prof. Osborn's Views."

The article explained that science had concluded that "severe restriction of immigration is essential to prevent the deterioration of American civilization." In the end, Osborn concluded that the Eugenics Congress was "perhaps the most important scientific meeting ever held in the Museum." And while Theodore Roosevelt had long argued the dangers of race suicide—the idea that the original founders of America were slowly losing ground to immigrants—Grant and Osborn dramatically expanded upon the idea.

Osborn would later summarize his racial beliefs in a 1924 article titled "Lo, the Poor Nordics." In it he discussed how the Nordics had first appeared in central Asia and then made their way into Europe around 12,000 BCE. Their struggle to overcome the adverse challenges of their environment, helped along by their genes, made them superior. They eventually gave rise to all the Europeans of distinction, and, according to Osborn, they included such notables as Da Vinci, Galileo, and Columbus. Ultimately, some of these Nordics crossed the Atlantic to continue their evolution in the New World. And as if to toss a few crumbs to all the other races, he finished the article by saying that all races produce great men, but that each race should celebrate its own, not "men who really belong to other races."

Although Osborn believed that the races were not all equal anatomically or spiritually, he did believe that there were quality non-Nordics who could contribute to American society, and that the improvement of all races benefited the country. He argued the fine line between selection and restriction, favoring the former, adding that he wanted "not more immigrants, but better immigrants." Osborn claimed that he wanted to cultivate the best from all races in America. He argued that "there were very good and desirable emigrants to be found in every country," and he criticized Grant for having too narrow and biased a view, which he thought would only prove detrimental in the long run.

In Akeley, Osborn saw someone who could be useful in teaching new immigrants American values by bringing them closer to nature. And in Andrews, Osborn saw someone capable of discovering his *Dawn Man* so that he could prove once and for all how man achieved its apex with the evolution of the Nordics. And in his Hall of the Age of Man, Osborn himself hoped to showcase the evidence for what he firmly believed was true.

CHAPTER SIXTEEN

The Gobi Desert

For the five months that Andrews roved the Gobi Desert while on the Central Asiatic Expedition in 1922, he was unable to communicate with the outside world. Not even Osborn knew whether the expedition was a failure or a success. There had been a complete news blackout, and so shortly after he got back to Peking, Andrews sent out a press release detailing everything he was sure the newspapers wanted to know "or at least ought to know." His goal was to inform the whole world of the expedition's success. "We had made scientific history," Andrews later explained, "and I wanted to get it into the public record as soon as possible."

Andrews was also eager to rebuke those who had doubted him. "I must say," he stated with satisfaction, "that those scientists who had been loudest in their prediction of failure were the first in admitting that they had been wrong." His idea to explore the desert with automobiles, supported by a caravan of camels laden with gasoline, food, and other supplies, had proven successful. Osborn responded with unabashed delight, pronouncing that the expedition had "written a new chapter in the history of life upon the earth." Similar messages came in from scientific and geographic societies around the world. "It was satisfying, to say the least,"

Andrews wrote, but left unsaid was the fact that he had not found the much-anticipated *Dawn Man*.

Spending the winter of 1922–1923 in Peking, Andrews and Yvette settled into their new home on Bowstring Street. Nestled at the rear of the expedition's headquarters, it was a sumptuous residential suite enclosed within a beautifully landscaped courtyard and decorated with ornately carved furniture and exquisite Asian art. Their son George would turn five while living there that winter, but what little time Andrews had for his family was too often interrupted by a steady stream of dinner invitations, cocktail parties, and sporting events with other members of the Western expatriate community. In an attempt to find some time for themselves, Andrews and Yvette rented a secluded temple in a rural area just outside Peking, but their relationship was already under strain. Consumed with his leadership of the expedition, Andrews more often than not left Yvette longing for companionship.

As for the Central Asiatic Expedition's second in command, Walter Granger spent the winter prospecting for fossils in China's conflict-ridden Szechuan Province. Steaming up the Yangtze River with his wife, Anna, they more than once found themselves ducking for cover as Chinese soldiers and warlords fired upon their passing junk. For their efforts they returned to Peking with baskets full of fossilized Cenozoic mammals, but still no *Dawn Man*.

Hardly a paleontologist himself, Andrews focused his attention on the living mammals of central Asia. He was especially interested in the big-game mammals that he could hunt—antelope, mountain goat, and the mysterious golden-fleeced takin—and in this way he effectively merged his passion for sport hunting with mammalogy. As he later explained, the living mammals were important in relation to the paleontology of Mongolia because they reinforced the same patterns of evolution seen in the fossils. It was all part of his plan to generate multiple lines of evidence in support of central Asia as the birthplace of mammalian life.

In the spring of 1923, the expedition readied for its second season in the Gobi, with the goal of returning to the Flaming Cliffs. Feeling a need for more fossil collectors, Granger had called in three more bone hunters from the United States, some of whom had experience working with the legendary Barnum Brown. Vehicle maintenance was another concern, and Andrews hired two mechanics, Mackenzie "Mac" Young and C. Vance Johnson, two men who had "lived with cars all their lives and were competent to repair any breakage which might result from the terrible punishment which we knew the motors would have to undergo." Andrews also promoted some of his Chinese staff, among them a mess boy named Kan Chuen-pao, whom everyone called Buckshot. He had proven himself so good at handling fossils that Granger made him a full-time field assistant. Altogether, the expedition's personnel increased to forty.

Led by the venerable Merin, the expedition's long line of two-humped camels departed Kalgan in early April, followed two weeks later by Andrews and the main expedition. A heavy snowfall slowed Andrews's progress, having turned the road leading into Mongolia into a "mass of gluelike mud," but on April 19 they passed through the Great Wall at Wanchuan on their way to Iren Dabasu, where they planned to meet the caravan with all their supplies. Bandits were known to be active in the region, and so Andrews grew concerned when he did not find them at their designated meeting point. Merin had planned to follow a trail that ran to the east of the main road, but none of the Mongols who had traveled that same route reported seeing him.

They waited a week, and Andrews feared Merin might have been ambushed and driven off into the desert. He was hardly reassured knowing that just a week before, two Russian cars loaded with furs had been ambushed by brigands disguised as Chinese soldiers. They stole everything from these traders and murdered one of them while leaving the rest stripped naked on the side of the road.

Andrews made up his mind to take aggressive action if his caravan was not heard from soon. He would "take three or four of our men who were simply spoiling for a fight, follow the caravan on horseback from the point where Merin had last been seen, and recapture it." But before he could act, news came that the caravan was safe and due to arrive in a matter of days. Having learned that brigands were watching the trail ahead of him, Merin had early on in his journey slipped off into the desert. He traveled only at night, camping during the day in sheltered hollows where the caravan could not be easily seen.

The expedition had safely reunited with their supply caravan when another obstacle arose. Word came that the Mongolian government, increasingly under the influence of Russian Bolshevik power, had broken its promise of support and was threatening to withhold the explorers' passports. Andrews was livid, and with characteristic bravado, threatened to drive to the seat of government in Urga himself in order to handle the matter by force. Fortunately, his Mongolian agents were able to smooth things over, but it was just the beginning of Andrews's troubles.

The Flaming Cliffs site was the focus of the 1923 expedition. Discovered in the last days of the previous year's field season, it was clearly the most promising. The site was littered with fossils eroding out of the cliffs, and the expedition had already brought back an unknown horned dinosaur skull that Granger named after Andrews. *Protoceratops andrewsi* was especially interesting because it was thought to be the earliest ancestor to the *Triceratops* that roamed the western part of North America during the Cretaceous. While on the way to the Flaming Cliffs, Granger hoped to visit some of the other sites from the previous year. Iren Dabasu was where they had stumbled upon both dinosaur and fossil mammal remains early on in the 1922 expedition, and Granger felt the site was the ideal place to introduce his newest paleontology recruits to Mongolia before penetrating deeper into the Gobi.

Not much of a fossil hunter himself, Andrews decided, along with C. Vance Johnson, to drive two cars back to Kalgan to pick up some supplies that had arrived too late to go with the caravan. Their trip went smoothly enough, but they encountered trouble on the way back. Andrews was driving about a mile ahead of Johnson when he caught a glint of sunlight on a rifle barrel. It came from a hilltop not far from where the two Russian cars had been robbed, and Andrews saw a horseman watching his approach through binoculars. Andrews guessed that the man was a brigand waiting to alert his companions hidden among the rocks, and so he drew his Colt .38 revolver and fired twice in the general direction of the horseman, not really trying to hit him. The rider suddenly vanished, but moments later, as the car topped the rim of the valley, Andrews saw three bandits at the base of the slope.

"It would have been difficult to turn the car and run without exposing myself to close-range shots," he later wrote, "and knowing that a Mongol pony would never stand against the charge of a motor car, I instantly decided to attack. The cut-out was wide and open and, with a smooth down-hill stretch in front of me, the car roared down the slope at forty miles an hour. The expected happened! While the brigands were attempting to un-ship their rifles which were slung on their backs, their horses went into a series of leaps and bounds, madly bucking and rearing with fright, so that the men could hardly stay in their saddles. In a second the situation had changed! The only thing the brigands wanted to do was get away, and they fled in panic. When I last saw them they were breaking all speed records on the other side of the valley."

Meanwhile, the paleontologists had excavated an extensive quarry of dinosaur skeletons of several different species all jumbled together at the Iren Dabasu site. Leaving some men there, the main body of the expedition moved on to a site they called the Valley of the Jewels, for the countless multicolored quartz pebbles that littered the ground. Here Buckshot found a beautifully preserved mammal skull three feet long. Andrews at once identified it as being a close relative of "the great carnivore *Mesonyx*, an odd looking creodont of gigantic size." He was right, and Osborn later named the new genus and species after the explorer—*Andrewsarchus mongoliensis*.

Keeping on the move, the expedition next spent two weeks at Ula Usu—Well of the Mountain Waters—where they excavated the skulls of several more titanotheres, the rhinoceros-like creatures that Osborn had studied in western North America. As Andrews would later note, "their discovery in Mongolia was the fulfillment of a brilliant prediction made by Prof. Osborn." For two decades he had been studying titanotheres, and although they were previously known only from North America, he predicted that they had originally been migrants from central Asia. Osborn had in fact instructed the expedition to be on the lookout for titanotheres, and they were among some of the first fossils found in the previous year. Ula Usu was "a veritable titanothere mine," Andrews wrote, and they would go on to collect fourteen skulls representing several different species from the site.

It was while they were at the Mountain Waters site that the expedition felt a stiff breeze and noticed an ominous dust cloud on the horizon. By afternoon the next day, the breeze had turned into a fierce gale, and the yellow clouds of dust became what Andrews described as "a thousand shrieking demons." It was their first experience with a sandstorm, and groping their way back to camp, they had to bury themselves under wet clothing in order to breathe through all the dust. One by one, everybody found their way back to camp, except for Granger, who had been caught out in the storm for several hours. Hours later, after the winds had subsided, he arrived back in camp caked with dirt. Looking at himself in a mirror, he remarked: "That finishes it. The Mongols have the right idea, no more baths for me. What's the use. I'm going to bed."

Having been in the field for months, the expedition prepared to finally move on to the Flaming Cliffs site, but Andrews was shocked to see how weak and emaciated the camels had become. They were woefully thin, with soft flapping humps. "It was imperative that the caravan reach the Flaming Cliffs with gasoline and food," he wrote, and so he chose the sixteen healthiest-looking camels and loaded them with just enough critical supplies to get them to the Flaming Cliffs. Not wanting to wait, Andrews planned to race ahead with his scientific team with just enough food and supplies to see them through until the caravan arrived. He was taking a real gamble. "If they did not reach us, the situation would be serious. Without gasoline we should be well-nigh as helpless as Robinson Crusoe on his desert island."

On July 3, the cars began the four-hundred-mile journey to the Flaming Cliffs, following in the same tracks that their cars had made the year before. The region was in the middle of a drought, and most of the inhabitants had since moved to greener pasturelands farther to the north, the skeletons of their weaker camels and sheep littering the sides of the track. The going was rough, and the cars kept sinking up to their axles in the parched sand. One truck finally had to be unloaded and carried up a long slope so that it could be used to pull all the others out, but they finally reached the Flaming Cliffs site on the afternoon of July 8. "Everything was exactly as we left it on our last visit," Andrews noted. "The marks of our tents and the motor car tracks were almost as distinct as though they had just been made." Their dark blue tents were once again arrayed in rows with the cars lined up to one side. Piles of metal boxes full of gasoline and scientific equipment lay everywhere. As soon as they arrived, they began excavating fossils. The place was full of *Protoceratops*, and after five weeks they had procured seventy skulls and fourteen skeletons seeming to represent every life stage possible.

The expedition's most impressive find, however, were three partially broken dinosaur eggs—the first dinosaur eggs known to science. Several days later they found more eggs, each about eight inches long, and inside two that were broken they found the fossilized remains of tiny embryos. The skulls of several infants were also found, suggesting that they, along with all the others, might have died together in something like the sudden sandstorm that the expedition had only recently experienced themselves.

As if fossil eggs were not enough, after clearing away the loose sediment from the ledge where the first eggs were found, they exposed the partial skeleton of a birdlike dinosaur which Osborn later named *Oviraptor*, meaning egg thief, because it appeared to have died in the act of raiding the nest of eggs. Overall, some twenty-five to thirty eggs were collected in 1923, and there seemed to be no doubt that they had been laid by *Protoceratops*.

While work continued at the Flaming Cliffs, Andrews and Mac Young went west to the peaks and ridges of the Altai Mountains to hunt bighorn sheep and ibex. After they returned, Andrews was worried because his supply caravan was still overdue. He rationed their remaining food, supplemented it with wild game, and saved the last of his gasoline for use in one car as an emergency supply. Besides food, they were also short on the burlap sheets they used for packing up their fossils, the standard procedure being to use flour paste reinforced with burlap to encase their fossils in a protective "jacket" for shipment. They had to jacket up fossils using bits of their own clothing. "There is in the collection," Andrews wrote, "a beautiful dinosaur skull fortified with strips from my pajamas."

As the days passed, Andrews grew increasingly alarmed at the prospect of being stranded as winter approached. Finally, he decided to send two of his most trusted Mongols on horseback to search for Merin. Within a few days one returned with nothing to report. The other, meanwhile, had traveled eastward so far that fodder for his horse became scarce. Leaving his steed at a nomad encampment, he bought a camel, and rode for a week without seeing another human. Then he had the misfortune of encountering two men who promptly attacked and robbed him. He was so savagely beaten that he could barely make his way to a temple to recover from his injuries. When he finally made it back to the Flaming Cliffs camp, he was nearly dead from starvation and thirst.

Meanwhile, Andrews was about to use up the last of their gasoline to lead a search party for the caravan when a wizened old Mongolian unexpectedly appeared in camp. "Our Mongols greeted him with the greatest reverence," Andrews recalled, "and told us that he was a famous astrologer who had heard of our predicament and had come more than thirty miles to help us. The Mongols said that he would be able to tell us exactly where the caravan was. [He] made elaborate preparations and, after a long incantation, announced that the caravan was many days' travel away from us, and that we would hear definite news of it in three days. He said that our camels were dying and that Merin was having a very difficult time. Our Mongols believed him implicitly."

As it turned out, the old man was fairly accurate in his assessment. Four days later they got news of Merin's whereabouts, and indeed he was sixty-five miles to the west, having lost many of his camels, but he eventually made it through, carrying enough gasoline and food to save the expedition. Packing up their fossils and zoological specimens, they filled sixty boxes containing five tons of specimens, all of them cushioned using shed fur from their camels.

As the expedition began their long journey back to Peking, they looked forward to a big event—a visit from Henry Fairfield Osborn. After months of planning, Osborn and his wife, Lucretia, were due to reach Shanghai in the first week of September, from where they were to proceed by train to Peking. Osborn's introduction to Mongolia was slated to occur at their Valley of the Jewels camp, followed by a visit to Iren Dabasu. Leaving Granger in charge of the expedition, Andrews and Mac Young raced back toward Kalgan, where they could catch a train to Peking to meet Osborn in time. When the two men arrived, they were met by Yvette, looking rather grim. "Never will I forget the shock I received as I stepped from the train in Peking," Andrews later recalled. It had been more than five months since he had last seen Yvette, and besides the fact that she was somewhere around five months pregnant—which came as a surprise to Andrews—she also had bad news about Osborn.

There had been a catastrophic earthquake, followed by fires and a tidal wave that devastated Yokohama and Tokyo the previous day.

Osborn's ship, the *President Jackson*, was supposedly anchored in Yokohama Harbor when the disaster struck. Nobody had heard from the ship, and its fate was unknown. Everyone feared the worst, and it was days before they got news that Osborn's ship had in fact sailed from Yokohama the day before the earthquake. Osborn, along with everyone else aboard the ship, knew nothing of their close call until they were informed of the disaster upon their arrival in Shanghai. Less fortunate was Mother Jesus, who was lost under the rubble of Number Nine, never to be seen again.

Osborn was enchanted by the expedition's Peking headquarters, with its quaint courtyards and exquisite art. Lucretia stayed behind at the compound with Yvette, while Andrews and Young whisked Osborn off to the desert the next day. Dressed in a hand-tailored bush jacket, knickerbockers, puttees, and a pith helmet, Osborn looked his usual stylish self as he posed for photographs in the desert.

"The trip was perfect," wrote Andrews. "At four o'clock in the golden sunshine of a Mongolian afternoon, we saw [our] blue tents swimming in the desert mirage. They hovered and danced on the heat waves in the air, finally settling to earth like great blue birds as we neared the camp. It was one of the greatest days of my life and of the expedition when the man, whose brilliant prediction had sent us into the field, stepped from the car at our camp in the desert." After tea, Osborn was driven to a pit where Granger had left a fossil jaw bone partly exposed for his inspection. "This," Osborn exclaimed, "is the high point of my scientific life."

Osborn would spend the next day digging fossils, and he also got to experience some added excitement when a group of armed bandits descended on their camp at night. Forewarned by the sentries Andrews had posted around camp, the scientists actually outgunned the bandits, and managed to surround them and bring them to submission. They were set free the next morning without their guns, and Andrews later learned that they had later been captured and shot by the Mongolian authorities.

On their last night in camp, Andrews and Osborn sat for an hour after dinner discussing the future of the expedition. Both men agreed that the challenge of exploring so immense an area that was so very rich in fossils was too much to be completed in just five years, and that something more like ten years would be necessary. They agreed to declare a recess in the field operations, and to start anew in 1925 so that Andrews would have some time to return to the United States to raise more money. Andrews would return to America without Yvette, who opted to stay behind in Peking, where months later she gave birth to another boy, the father of whom perhaps only she knew for certain.

CHAPTER SEVENTEEN

Snake Eyes

Andrews returned to the United States to find news of his recent expedition all around him. "Dinosaur eggs! Dinosaur eggs!" That was all Andrews heard for eight months after his return. It was as if people were expecting the eggs to hatch, he remarked. The newspapers could not get enough of Roy Chapman Andrews, an alluring mix of scientist and socialite. More than four thousand people showed up for his first public lecture at the museum, and Andrews had to give back-to-back talks to accommodate them all. The man was a star. Featured in such magazines as *The Saturday Evening Post*, *Harper's*, and *Cosmopolitan*, Andrews reached the height of his personal fame when his portrait appeared on the cover of *Time* magazine in October 1923.

Whenever he was in New York, Andrews stayed at Osborn's town house at 998 Fifth Avenue. He was one of the few nonfamily members to have such privilege, and it was during breakfast one morning that Andrews and Osborn started talking about fundraising. They had already raised a quarter of a million dollars since their return from Mongolia, but Andrews was sure he could raise more. But rather than hobnobbing with his usual donors over cigars and cocktails, Andrews wanted to tap ordinary Americans. Up until that time, sponsoring an expedition seemed a rich man's pleasure, but Andrews thought it might be time for a change. It was then that he got the idea to auction off one of the eggs. As a publicity stunt, Andrews felt it might spur the public to donate money. Seeking more than just the proceeds from the sale, he thought it would set off an avalanche of smaller donations. Regardless, the ploy had the immediate effect of tainting the Central Asiatic Expeditions as something of a moneymaking venture.

Andrews realized his mistake at once, as some forty reporters crammed into his office at the museum to hear about the scheme. Yes, one egg would be sold to the highest bidder, Andrews confirmed. Invitations to bid had been sent to some very high-profile museums, including the Smithsonian Institution. The "Great Dinosaur Egg Auction" eventually did spur everyday folks to donate, but Andrews forever regretted the scheme because of its unintended consequences. "Up to this time the Chinese and Mongols had taken us at face value," Andrews later wrote. "Now they thought we were making money out of our explorations." In the end, they only got $5,000 from someone who promptly donated the egg to Colgate University.

Andrews also suffered consequences from having signed some lucrative sponsorship deals. The most important of these was with the Dodge Motor Company, which agreed to provide a new fleet of cars for the 1925 expedition. Having a famous explorer like Andrews drive their cars around the Gobi was great publicity, and the company offered to supply five cars, among them a sleek open-top touring car for Andrews to cruise around in while doing desert reconnaissance. Andrews later arranged similar deals with Eveready flashlights, Smith-Corona typewriters, and Savage Arms. He insisted that these deals were all "entirely legitimate," stressing that he simply endorsed the products that worked out well for him in the field, but not everyone was so sure.

Meanwhile, Andrews went on a whirlwind lecture tour across the country. Virtually every day, and sometimes two or three times a day, he was busy giving talks. During four months on the road, he appeared before 125 audiences. When it was all over, he could only remark that he felt like a "sucked orange." All but forgotten was Yvette, who on January 20, 1924, had given birth in Peking to a second son, Roy Kevin Andrews. Incredibly, it would be another five months before Andrews would return to Peking to see the boy.

Even in the 1920s, museums were not at liberty to just barge into foreign countries for the purposes of collecting specimens. Then as now, permissions had to be negotiated well in advance of any fieldwork, and so on August 25, 1924, Andrews arrived in Urga, Mongolia, to find it a very different place. Mongolia was fast becoming a hotbed of intrigue, as Bolshevik ideology began to be imported from Moscow. Secret police were everywhere, there was a climate of fear, and foreigners especially were viewed with suspicion. It was only because Andrews had nurtured the support and respect of some highly effective Mongol facilitators—men who were willing to take risks for him—that he was able to negotiate permissions for the expedition. Or so he thought.

On a bitterly cold morning in February, Andrews set the 1925 Central Asiatic Expedition in motion when he sent Merin, and the expedition's hundred-plus camel caravan, on a journey of more than eight hundred miles into the desert. Assuming all went well, Andrews hoped to see him again at the Flaming Cliffs later that spring. As with the two previous expeditions, the success of the entire expedition depended on Merin getting their necessary supplies into the interior, and Andrews was confident in Merin's ability to withstand cold and avoid the brigands who roamed the desolate expanses. These and many other hardships had been a part of Merin's life since childhood.

As members of the 1925 expedition arrived in Peking in the spring, Andrews welcomed Nels C. Nelson, a Danish-born archeologist. Charged with finding evidence of ancient man, he was just one of fourteen scientists and technicians, eleven Chinese cooks, taxidermists, camp assistants, and some fourteen Mongol interpreters and caravanners on their team. They had one Dodge touring vehicle, four three-quarter-ton cars, and two one-ton Fulton trucks. Somewhere out in the desert was their caravan of 125 camels carrying four thousand gallons of gasoline in sealed cans, one hundred gallons of oil, and several dozen spare tires. For food they had two and a half tons of flour, a ton of rice, half a ton of sugar, and an equally prodigious selection of canned goods.

Racing across the Mongolian grasslands, their vehicles piled high with gear, they were a mere two hundred miles into their journey when Andrews spied a Mongol waving a red sash on the summit of a hill. The man galloped toward them on a rangy camel with the news that Merin and the entire caravan had been captured by some soldiers who had confiscated all their supplies. Andrews was furious because the Mongolian government in the capital at Urga had given him a special permit to move his camels across the border without duty or inspection. But such papers meant little to a soldier on the frontier, and Andrews suspected they were holding out for a bribe. Calling the Mongolians an "insolent breed of petty officials," Andrews went on to explain how "every Chinese caravan has pitiful tales of their activities in this respect!" But more than money, Andrews was worried about lost time.

As he advanced toward where Merin was being held, Andrews interviewed passing nomads. Rumor had it the caravan was being held because it contained ammunition, which was true, but Andrews also heard some snippets about some soldiers who were supposedly waiting to ambush him along the trail. Some claimed these soldiers were under orders to have Andrews shot.

Still some eighty miles from where the caravan was being detained, Andrews paused at his old Well of the Waters site. He would leave the bulk of the expedition here to begin their fossil hunting while he and five other men resolved to free Merin. As Andrews rationalized it, he could either stand up for the validity of his permissions from the government officials in Urga, or abandon the expedition entirely. "I was certain that a show of force would quickly intimidate the ignorant wretches who are accustomed to bullying the helpless Chinese but we were determined 'to go to the limit' if necessary." True to his words, when Andrews and his men encountered those soldiers who were waiting to arrest him, they "treated them with scant courtesy." One of the soldiers Andrews described as being "bundled unceremoniously into the car" and Andrews ordered him to direct them to the place where the caravan was being held.

Andrews found Merin held amidst a collection of felt-covered yurts arrayed around one large yurt in the center. A hundred yards away he saw an American flag flying over Merin's tent, which had a long line of boxes and camels impounded beside it. "Our Mongols welcomed us like joyous children," Andrews noted. Five minutes later, Andrews was notified that he was under arrest and that he would be taken to Urga at once. Told that the head man would call for them when it was time to go, and that the cars should not move from where they had stopped, Andrews's response was swift and decisive: "Tell your chief that *we* are ready to see him *now*," and then following closely on the messenger's heels all six of them approached the yurt. "I pulled up the felt door-flap and stepped inside followed by Granger, Young, Lovell and two of our Mongols. A circle of twenty Mongols and Buryats sat staring at us in fascinated silence. I said nothing for a few moments, then suddenly demanded, "Who is the head man?" A man at the far end of the yurt, wearing a gorgeous yellow satin coat and a sable-bordered hat, slowly raised his hand. "How dare you ignore the passport of your government and hold our caravan?" Andrews asked. "You are a bandit. Explain instantly."

From the moment of Andrews's arrival, the man had been taken aback by Andrews's belligerent attitude. He was running a string of prayer beads through his hand faster and faster as Andrews confronted him. Finally, he managed to stammer that he wanted to pass the caravan but that his soldier colleague would not do so because it contained ammunition, and also such dangerous and seditious literature as *The Saturday Evening Post*, among other American magazines.

As further evidence, he pointed to a large box of flashlight batteries that he was certain had to be bombs.

The men listened in silence, and then Andrews made a tremendous bang with his fist on the stove that made every man in the yurt jump. Andrews pointed out that they had ignored the government permit to allow the caravan to pass no matter what it contained, and that they had ruined many of their supplies and that *they* intended to take *him* to Urga to answer for what he had done. By the end of it, the captors were so frightened they just wanted Andrews, Merin, and his caravan to leave. As Andrews later described it, "We could cheerfully have beaten every man there within an inch of his life but that would only have created trouble for the future." Instead, they rustled up their camels and got on with the expedition, now seriously delayed and with many of their camels dangerously weakened.

From the Well of the Waters, the expedition headed southwest across the trackless plains, stopping here and there to examine promising rock outcrops. Andrews continued his studies of Mongolia's living animals, trapping and shooting birds and mammals, which the Chinese taxidermists skinned and prepared as museum study specimens. When they finally reached the Flaming Cliffs, Nels Nelson, the archeologist, was quick to discover all kinds of artifacts—stone hammers, axes, scrapers, and arrow points, along with knives and blades made out of chert and other stones. For a moment, Andrews might have thought he had finally found evidence of his *Dawn Man*, but none of these human artifacts were of any great age. As Nelson explained, the many thousands of artifacts they recovered all seemed to range in age from the late Paleolithic to Neolithic times. They were far too recent to belong to the ancestors of all humanity. These were the remains of mere Stone Age men, and since all the artifacts had been found on the exposed hard ground between shifting sand dunes, they called the unknown people the Dune Dwellers.

Every day that they stayed at the Flaming Cliffs site, members of the expedition found fossils—*Protoceratops* skulls in abundance, and still more dinosaur eggs—and Andrews remained hopeful that they might soon find older human ancestors. He liked to sit and look at the towering rocks that had been shaped by wind and sand for millennia. "Like a fairy city it is ever-changing," he wrote. "In the flat light of midday the strange forms shrink and lose their shape; but when the sun is low the Flaming Cliffs assume a deeper red, and a wild mysterious beauty lies with the purple shadows in every canyon."

On Andrews's mind, however, was the sorry state of his supply caravan. Out of the 125 camels that the expedition had started out with, only 85 still survived, the rest having died along the way. More foreboding news came when a messenger arrived in camp calling Andrews back to Urga at once. "New government regulations had been passed," the messenger said, "which required discussion if we were to continue our explorations." Andrews would have to travel all the way back to the capital city of Mongolia.

A storm was stirring on the horizon as Andrews and Young left for Urga in late May, taking one car and their most reliable interpreter. The storm drew closer as they drove, kicking up a wall of gravel and yellow-brown sand. Stopping at the yurt of some welcoming nomads, they warmed themselves over a blazing dung-fueled fire before setting up their tent with the opening facing away from the approaching storm, now a blizzard of blinding snow. But the winds shifted in the night, and when they awakened their tent was filled with snow. "All our clothes," Andrews wrote, "were deeply buried."

Still three hundred more miles from their destination, their progress was slowed by snow drifts covering hidden gullies. Again and again, the car had to be dug out and jacked up so that rocks could be placed under the wheels in order to move it. They spent the next night in another yurt, sharing it with two Mongols, their baby, and a foul-smelling goat and some calves. After suffering all these ordeals, they came upon the beautiful sight of Urga the next morning. "Peaceful enough it looked in the spring sunshine, but I knew that it was a city of suspicion, and one not to be entered without due thought of how one was to get out," Andrews recalled.

Perhaps the Mongolian officials had come to regret the agreement they had made with the American Museum to prospect for fossils? Or maybe it was because of the growing influence of Russian political operatives in their country? No matter the reason, it was clear to everyone that the Mongolian officials wished to reassert control over the AMNH expedition. At first, Andrews was asked to tend to some matters in the local museum, and so he and Young helped install a *Protoceratops* skeleton and a nest of dinosaur eggs for exhibit. This was all in accordance with the original agreement they had signed in 1922, but even as they performed these tasks they were subjected to a "merciless searching of our persons." Andrews complained about how "every scrap of writing and all books were sent to the Secret Service office to be perused by censors." By the end of it, they were told that the working arrangements and permissions they had negotiated the year before had been nullified, and that new regulations tailored especially for Andrews's expedition were now in effect.

Andrews was sure it was payback for his auctioning off one egg the year before, and there came a long list of impossible demands. Among these new rules, they were now told that they had to bring all their specimens to Urga so that the Scientific Committee could pick out anything they wanted. They were not permitted to make any more maps, and they could not engage in any kind of geological work, nor could they use any kind of radio. They were to accept two Mongol government-appointed students who were to be sent to America to be educated at Harvard. Finally, two government agents were to accompany the expedition so that they could send back regular reports on the expedition's activities, and one of the agents had to be from the secret police.

After days of negotiations, and with the help of his Mongol

collaborators, Andrews was able to get the most egregious of these new restrictions rescinded, but not the two agents, whom he begrudgingly accepted as members of the expedition. When they finally left the city two weeks later, these two agents bounced along in the back of the car as they sped back to their camp. Still, Andrews could not help but see these new developments as a sign of troubles to come. The Communists were tightening their grip on Mongolia, and Andrews knew that it was just a matter of time before he was kicked out of Mongolia for good.

Gone for two weeks by the time Andrews and Young rejoined the expedition, Granger had already sent the camel caravan ahead to their next rendezvous site, but they were still digging up good fossils, among them some small but ancient primitive mammal skulls. Barely an inch long, Andrews thought they were "among the most precious of all the remarkable specimens that we obtained in Mongolia." They represented some of the earliest known mammals from the Cretaceous period, and had existed alongside the dinosaurs, offering clues to the origins and evolution of mammals. If Osborn's concept of the Asian origins of mammals were to be proved, these were just the sorts of fossils they needed most. They collected samples representing some of the earliest examples of marsupials and shrews, yet the fossil primates they most desired remained elusive.

Their work at the Flaming Cliffs nearing its end, Andrews grew restless. He took an excursion to the south, driving off to explore the foothills of the Altai Mountains. Even though he had been warned by some of the Mongols of difficult terrain, he could not help but push southward toward the distant mountains. Driven to find his *Dawn Man*, Andrews was forever pushing the limits of the expedition. Unable to punch through, Andrews described the "massive ramparts" of the Altai as "banning us from the south." Full of canyons and dry streambeds, the terrain was "passable for horses and camels without a doubt," but to Andrews's dismay, it was "but hopeless for cars."

Returning to the Flaming Cliffs, and with rumors of war with China and the increasing hostility of the Mongolians on his mind, Andrews took one last look at the site. "This single spot," he later reflected, "had given us more than we dared to hope for from the entire Gobi. . . . I was filled with regret as I looked for the last time at Flaming Cliffs, gorgeous in the morning sunshine of the brilliant August day. I suppose I shall never see them again!"

A chilly north wind blew, and aware of the suddenness with which the Mongolian winter arrived, Andrews turned the expedition toward home. They would continue to collect fossils as they slowly worked their way back to Kalgan, but in their last camp, they had an ominous experience. Roy Chapman Andrews hated snakes, and found three of them waiting for him close to the entrance of his tent. He recognized the brown, mottled serpents as pit vipers similar to the North American copperhead, and highly venomous. They had encountered a few snakes before during the course of their expedition, but suddenly others were having snake encounters in camp, too. It was as if nature was conspiring against Andrews and trying to evict him from Mongolia—his mad quest for the *Dawn Man* an insult to the very nature of the place.

The sun went down and a sudden rapid drop in temperature brought more snakes slithering into camp. Drawn to the warmth of the men's bodies, the snakes entered their camp in droves, causing everyone "a very busy night." Within a matter of minutes, all the tents were alive with snakes. One expedition member saw one slithering through his doorway, but before leaping out of bed to kill it, he wisely checked the floor beside his bed with a flashlight. Wrapped around all four legs of his cot were vipers, which he one by one bashed with his geologist's pick. Another snake slithered out from under a gasoline tin near his head, and he disposed of several more, while others killed nearly as many in their own tents.

One of the Chinese drivers found a viper coiled in his shoe, and another fell out of his hat. Soon many of them were dashing for the safety of the car to spend the night. Armed with a hatchet, Andrews attacked something soft and round under his foot only to discover that it was a piece of rope. Moments later, Granger lunged savagely at what turned out to be a pipe cleaner.

Forty-seven vipers were killed that night. It was definitely time to go home.

CHAPTER EIGHTEEN

The Most Beautiful Place

Osborn made it clear from the beginning that he expected Akeley to raise his own funds for Africa Hall. As president of the museum, he was willing to plug for new buildings but not expensive expeditions. He had already committed the museum to the Central Asiatic Expeditions, which *still* hadn't found his *Dawn Man*, so if Akeley ever wanted to get back to Africa, he had to raise the money on his own.

Taking his idea outside New York, Akeley traveled the country on a lecture tour. Everywhere he went, he told of his dream to build a great hall of African mammals at the American Museum. In convincing tones, he spoke of how its future majesty would once and for all destroy the myth of Africa as a place of gloomy forests and ferocious beasts. Such were the tales of Du Chaillu and explorers of old, but Akeley described Africa as an enchanting place.

Determined to advance his cause, Akeley wrote magazine articles, and with the help of a ghostwriter named Dorothy S. Greene, published his autobiography in a book called *In Brightest Africa*. Above all else, Akeley wished to portray the continent as something other than a place of darkness. In the mountain home of the gorilla was where Akeley wanted to be, as he desperately sought to complete his memorial to the great fauna of Africa.

Despite his passion, Akeley was hardly an effective fundraiser. He was too intense, and lacked the charm needed to put a donor at ease. "Akeley will kill himself before the project will come to completion," Osborn once confided to Andrews over breakfast. "Won't you talk to him and see what you can do?"

As things turned out, Akeley and Andrews were already crossing paths. Years before, Andrews had befriended the filmmakers Martin and Osa Johnson—creators of the hits *Jungle Adventures* (1921) and *Headhunters of the South Seas* (1922)—and they were already in negotiations with *Asia* magazine to film Andrews in the Gobi Desert. That's when Akeley stepped in and convinced them to work with him in Africa instead. Andrews expressed only slight disappointment when he heard this news, thinking it just as well to not turn his expedition into a "motion picture show."

A motion picture photographer himself, Akeley felt that the Johnsons' films might help popularize Africa, and with Osborn's consent, offered them the backing of the American Museum's prestigious name. Martin Johnson loved the idea—it was free publicity—but Akeley got very little out of the deal in return. All he wanted to do was promote the idea of Africa, believing it would one day lead to greater enthusiasm for his exhibit.

Frustrated with Akeley's lack of results, and leery of too obviously crossing mass entertainment with serious science, Osborn finally appointed David Pomeroy, a prominent New York banker and museum trustee, to step in and take charge of Akeley's fundraising. Pomeroy then created an independent entity called the Martin Johnson African Expedition Corporation, which he headed, and which he used to lure his friend George Eastman, the founder of the Eastman Kodak photographic empire, into the museum's sphere.

Eastman happened to be an avid big-game hunter, but at the age of seventy-one, he had never been to Africa. Pomeroy enticed him with the possibility of hunting with Carl Akeley and collecting animals for his exhibit. As Pomeroy explained it, Eastman had the opportunity to hunt for a good cause, and when he mentioned that the filmmakers Martin and Osa Johnson might also come along, Eastman wanted to hear more.

Taking a night train up to see Eastman in Rochester, Akeley told Pomeroy exactly what he was going to do when they got there. "I'd like to see Mr. Eastman give a million dollars." It was typical Akeley bluntness, and Pomeroy suggested a subtler approach. Perhaps he should describe his vision for Africa Hall in picturesque detail first, he suggested, but when he actually came face-to-face with his prospective sponsor, Akeley was soon stumbling over his words . . . *there was no money . . . it was up to him . . . it would be the greatest exhibit in the world.* And as if facing some charging elephant, Akeley then snapped the trigger—*he needed nothing less than one million dollars.*

Eastman was stunned, and later confided to Pomeroy that he was not prepared to give quite so much. "Would one hundred thousand dollars suffice?" he asked. It was more than enough to get them started, and after Pomeroy contributed some funds, too, the Akeley-Eastman-Pomeroy Expedition of 1926–1927 was born. Departing Rochester for New York, Akeley said to Pomeroy, "This is the most wonderful thing that has ever happened. At last I begin to see the realization of my life dream. At last!"

Carl Akeley's Africa Hall would be built in a new section of the museum with broad entrances at either end. It would be a vast and unobstructed hall full of glass windows through which the African habitat groups would be viewed. He would mount the most spectacular mammals of Africa in lifelike poses using the taxidermy methods he perfected, and he would place them amidst such natural settings as to convey the African wilderness of old. There would be forty such scenes in all, twenty on the ground floor, and twenty more on a mezzanine level above. This was a significant aggrandizement of what he had originally envisioned for the hall. Each group would have a painted background depicting the exact habitat of the animals displayed, and altogether these varied backgrounds would give a comprehensive idea of the scenery of Africa. It would be "an everlasting monument to the Africa that was, the Africa that is now fast disappearing."

Meanwhile, Osborn was successful in raising money for a new building to house Africa Hall, which would be joined to a rotunda on the Central Park side of the museum that would serve as a monument to Theodore Roosevelt. The construction of these buildings was set to proceed just as Akeley was preparing to go to Africa, and Osborn urged him to pull together a temporary exhibit before his departure. Motivated by the certain reality of Africa Hall, Akeley took the four taxidermy elephants and all his mountain gorillas, and arranged them as an ensemble that vaguely represented the basic idea of Africa Hall. These would hold the public's interest while Akeley was in the field.

Next, Akeley selected the members of his expedition, the most important of whom was the taxidermist Robert H. Rockwell, a Ward's graduate best known for having mounted a number of the animals shot by Theodore Roosevelt in East Africa for the Smithsonian. He had only just started working with James Clark in the taxidermy studio at the American Museum when he was called to join the expedition. To assist Rockwell, they hired the technician Richard Raddatz, whom Akeley had known since his Field Museum days.

When Rockwell asked Akeley what he might need most beside his Springfield rifle and old hunting clothes, Akeley chuckled and replied: "Just take your rifle and ammunition," before adding that in Africa, the hunting dress code was a little different from what Rockwell was accustomed to in the United States. "Yes indeed, you have to dress up to hunt in Africa," Akeley said, before explaining how he would need to buy khaki suits, a pith helmet, and spiral puttees to protect his legs against insects. "You'll also want a good Burberry raincoat, and most important of all—a tuxedo for special functions."

Rockwell burst out laughing, but Akeley cut him short. "No, no, I mean it. A tuxedo is a must."

For the first time ever, Akeley would be taking a couple of landscape painters along to capture the awesome scenery of Africa. They would make reference paintings that would later be translated into the curved panoramic backgrounds for each of the dioramas. After careful consideration, Akeley chose the artist William R. Leigh, who was well-known as the Sagebrush Rembrandt for his panoramic paintings of Western scenery, and the Grand Canyon especially. To assist him, they recruited Arthur A. Jansson, a very capable artist on the museum staff.

Once in the field, the expedition would be joined by Martin and Osa Johnson, George Eastman, and Daniel Pomeroy. Finally, there was Mary Jobe Akeley, the American mountaineer and explorer of the Rockies, and Carl's new wife. Although hesitant at first, she agreed to abandon her own career and interests to follow Akeley in the field.

The weeks and months of preparation before the expedition were some of the happiest of Akeley's life. Preoccupied with his mission, he became absent-minded. He would forget to put gasoline in his car and would stall in Fifth Avenue traffic, or he would leave his car unlocked, and later find that his spare tire was stolen. For weeks prior to their departure, he spoke joyously to Mary Jobe of the happy day when he would finally lead her and his artists into the glorious forests atop the Virunga volcanoes. As the day of their departure neared, Mary Jobe captured his spirit in a quote, later published in her own account of their adventure:

"Today I am again preparing to enter Africa. The forthcoming expedition means more to me than any that has gone before, not merely because it enables me to return to the country I love, but because it is the actual beginning of Africa Hall—the realization of my fondest dream. I am always dreaming dreams; many of them have been forgotten. But the dream of Africa Hall—of a great museum exhibition, artistic in form, permanent in construction, faithful to the scenery and the wild life of the continent it portrays—that dream has lived to become the unifying purpose of my work. Soon I shall be on my way to Africa, this time accompanied by artists and taxidermists, happy in the knowledge that my years of preparation are ended and my big work actually begun!"

Finally, on January 30, 1926, Carl and Mary departed for Africa, but even before they left New York, Carl seemed haggard. Stooped and graying, he was sixty-two years old. This would be his fifth expedition to Africa, and the years had certainly taken their toll. He had been mauled by a leopard in 1895, and nearly crushed to death by an elephant in 1910, but it was the steady strain of his relentless efforts that really wore him down. It had been thirteen years since the museum first approved his plans for Africa Hall, and after so many false starts, this sudden call to action was both thrilling and exhausting.

Arriving in London, they stayed only a few days to finish ordering supplies before traveling on to Belgium. There Akeley had been invited by Belgium's King Albert to discuss the specifics of the gorilla sanctuary he had proposed years before. It was agreed that while he was in the Belgian Congo, Akeley would be accompanied by the king's representative, Jean Marie Derscheid, a zoologist tasked with exploring and mapping the topography of the three Virunga volcanoes on which the Parc National Albert was to be located. He would work with Akeley to make a general survey of the gorilla population around the volcanoes.

After they arrived in Nairobi, Carl and Mary rented a house in the suburb of Parklands as the expedition's headquarters, but they themselves stayed in the Norfolk Hotel. There Akeley was reunited with many of his old friends from Africa, among them his trusty gun bearer "Bill," now very much a successful hunting guide and "fixer" for European and American clients.

Meeting his two artists in Mombasa a few weeks later, Akeley wanted to get them in the field right away. He was anxious to start the work of the expedition, and had selected the Lukenia Hills as their first destination—a beautiful rock-studded expanse overlooking the Athi Plains just forty miles east of Nairobi. There they made a camp with breathtaking views of glacier-topped Mt. Kenya to the northwest, and the summit of Mt. Kilimanjaro to the south. The site was to be the focus of Akeley's klipspringer diorama. These tiny antelope, which live as monogamous pairs atop rocky outcrops, are highly territorial, and spend their days bounding atop the rocks on the tips of their blunt hooves. They were easy to observe, and the site was ideal for getting the two artists accustomed to working in Africa.

In the Lukenia Hills, Leigh and Jansson got right to work painting the scenery. They needed to take a great deal of care to ensure that the diorama would be an accurate re-creation of the site. Using an old crate, Akeley crafted a scale model of the klipspringer diorama on the spot, adding bits of vegetation and sculpting little animals out of clay to fill out the composition. This needed to be done on location, where Akeley could take into consideration all the possible elements in composing a scene. As they worked in plein air, each of the artists was guarded by one of their gun bearers, so that they could concentrate on their painting without having to worry about looking over their shoulders for lions.

Meanwhile, Eastman, Pomeroy, and Rockwell arrived in Nairobi, where they were first met by Mary Jobe. Akeley arrived shortly afterward to find that Eastman was in a sour mood. "He had no capacity for conviviality, and was an extremely hard man to get to know," Rockwell commented about Eastman. It was the wet season, and as the heavy rains made many of the roads impassable, Eastman was chafed about not being able to hunt. They had to make special arrangements for Eastman to hunt in the Kidong Valley while Akeley took Rockwell back to the Lukenia Hills camp.

Back on site, "Akeley worked like a demon," Rockwell later recalled. "Every hour of the day he toiled and at night he would still be busy developing films, even though obviously fatigued. He often rose at four in the morning to take panorama pictures of Mount Kenya as the sun first struck its magnificent peaks with rays of gold and pink. It was too long a day for a man of his years and I marveled at how he was able to do it."

Unbeknownst to most members of the team, Akeley was still short of money, and with it growing increasingly clear that Eastman was not going to help out, he became grumpy. It was also disheartening for Akeley to see how much Africa had changed in the five years since his last visit. The land was not nearly as wild as he had remembered, the great herds of game supplanted by the encroachment of towns and cultivated fields. Perhaps also on Akeley's mind was the fact that he was not getting any younger himself, and that he might have to entrust the completion of Africa Hall to others.

Six weeks in the Lukenia Hills were enough for them to make all the study paintings they needed, and in addition, Rockwell and Raddatz had collected samples of plants, making impressions of their leaves to be molded into wax re-creations back at the museum. Akeley had finished his little model of the klipspringer group, complete with a miniature backdrop painting. Most important of all, he had collected, measured, skinned, and salted the skins of the four klipspringers he would later mount for the exhibit. The animals being rather small, and the scenery pleasant, Lukenia was the perfect place for the members of the expedition to learn what was required of them and to start working together as a team.

Next, the expedition moved on to the arid region north of Mt. Kenya, where amidst the flat-topped acacia trees they collected material for a planned water hole group in the northeast corner of Africa Hall. On their list of animals to procure were zebra, gazelle, and oryx, but Akeley wanted a family of three giraffe as the diorama's main feature. What's more, he was adamant that the big male of the group be no less than sixteen feet tall. He wanted the animal to exactly fit the available space back at the museum. This was easy enough for

Akeley to decree, but as Rockwell later explained, they saw plenty of smaller giraffe every day, and taking one of them would have been as easy as "going out on a cattle ranch and shooting down a steer," but it was days before they finally found a suitable sixteen-foot-tall specimen to shoot.

Akeley magnanimously allowed Rockwell the shot, but he carried a relatively small 30-30 rifle more suited for deer in America. Rockwell aimed and took the shot, and while the big giraffe was clearly hit, it did not go down. Speeding across the grassy plain in their open-top Chevrolet, clouds of dust kicked up behind them as Akeley fired off a fusillade of bullets, emptying his rifle in the process. Grabbing his elephant gun as they sped up alongside the loping giraffe, Akeley was poised to finish it off with a shot to the head when it finally dropped. It measured just over sixteen feet tall, and after taking a series of reference photos and some sixty body measurements, they prepared to skin it where it lay.

Using poles and ropes, they first strung a tarpaulin over the carcass to protect it from the scorching sun, and then they spent hours skinning and salting the hide. Rubbing the salt into the hide with his bare hands, Akeley was rather astonished to see that for all his shooting, only one bullet had penetrated the body, and that was the shot from Rockwell. Sometime later, one of the Africans helping to strip flesh from the skeleton, which was saved in addition to the skin, walked up to Rockwell with his hand outstretched. "The bullet from your little gun," he said to Rockwell. From then on Akeley let Rockwell do more of the hunting, and three weeks later he had secured a female giraffe and a youngster to complete the family group.

Leaving the artists behind to finish their work, Akeley and the hunters moved on to the Serengeti, where one of their missions was to collect animals for a plains animal group, but a second mission was to collaborate with Martin Johnson on making a motion picture of a native lion-spearing ritual, as performed by the men of a local Lumbwe tribe. Akeley had seen such spectacles before, but had never been able to film them, and spent days at the Serengeti camp rigging one of his own Akeley cameras to his Chevrolet. Martin Johnson did the same. This way they could motor across the plains while filming all the action. An entire village of men turned out, and for two weeks beginning on August 2, they made movies of the tribesmen hunting lions.

Later, Bill brought them to another place where lions had not been much hunted, and this offered a great opportunity for still more filming. They made superb close-up films of the prides, and much as Akeley had once persuaded his first wife, Delia, to shoot an elephant, he insisted that Mary Jobe partake of this same rite of passage by bagging a trophy lion. She did it, but it was the first and last animal she ever hunted.

One afternoon, while returning from one of these photographic trips, Akeley spotted a group of wild dogs on the horizon. Beautiful animals with splotches of black, orange, and white fur, they are highly social hunters, but also quite savage. Like hyena, they relentlessly pursue their prey to exhaustion before disemboweling and eating the hapless animal alive. Akeley wanted the dogs for Africa Hall, and he urged Mary to speed after them as they raced across the open plains. "Nine dogs, eight shots, seven minutes," was how Bill described the results. Akeley had shot one of the dogs, and the bullet had gone through to kill another.

Collecting all the dead dogs and throwing them in the back of the car, Akeley felt the beginnings of a distinct weariness. Skinning the dogs back in camp, he was terribly fatigued, and afterward went to his tent with a high fever. From time to time, he would stagger out to try to get something done, but his fever only intensified. Making matters worse, there was a raging brushfire to the north of their camp, and the smoky haze burned everyone's eyes and lungs. Finally, Mary Jobe and Pomeroy decided they had no choice but to evacuate Akeley to Nairobi for medical attention.

They arranged Akeley's bed in the back of a truck, and for three days they drove him over rough roads to the city. Along the way, Akeley directed them to stop in the Kidong Valley, where Rockwell had gone to do some collecting. As Akeley emerged from his ambulance to greet him, Rockwell was shocked by his "drawn, emaciated appearance . . . his once powerful hands were thin, with the tendons showing plainly." Akeley explained how he was not well—clearly apparent from his ghastly appearance—and then outlined all the work he wanted Rockwell to do during his convalescence.

Although Mary had wired ahead to request a room in Nairobi Hospital, when they arrived, the place was full, so she had to take him to the Kenya Nursing Home instead. There a doctor diagnosed his illness as "complete exhaustion from strain and overwork." Akeley spent three weeks in the nursing home, and as his condition seemed to improve, he moved into the Parklands house to continue his recovery. While he rested, various members of the expedition awaited further instructions. Akeley was supposed to go hunting for kudu with Pomeroy, but he abandoned that plan in order to focus all his attention on getting back into the Belgian Congo.

More than anything else, Akeley wanted to return to the site on Mt. Mikeno where he had shot his gorillas years before, and was eager to get started. All four animals—the lone male of Karisimbi chief among them—were already mounted and waiting at the American Museum. All he needed now was for the artists to make their studies for the background painting, and for Raddatz to collect plants and make molds of the vegetation so they could reproduce them in wax for the diorama.

But there was also a more personal reason for why Akeley wanted to get back to the mountain, and it was because he remembered the cool moist upper slopes of Mt. Mikeno as the most enchanting place in the world, with its thick moss and festoons of epiphytic vines. It was a magical place for Akeley. It was as if that one scene—so hard to reach, but well worth the effort—encapsulated all his feelings for Africa and what he envisioned for Africa Hall. Even before he and Mary Jobe had left for Africa, Akeley had hinted that he might not live to see his beloved Africa Hall completed. Years of work would be needed to complete the forty dioramas Akeley envisioned, but he was not sure he had that much time. If only he could get his crew to that site high up on Mikeno, where the trees, moss, and vines all converged against the backdrop of the valley for a perfect composition, he felt that at least he could convey the very essence of what he wanted Africa Hall to evoke. Everything rested on getting his team to that one magical spot on Mikeno—no other spot would do—before Akeley could rest knowing he had passed on the very spirit of what he felt in his heart. His life's work may have depended on killing individual animals, but his real motivation was to save them, through the transcendent beauty of his creation.

He called on Derscheid, the Belgian zoologist, to tell him he was ready to get on with their survey. He wanted to help him establish the gorilla sanctuary he had planned many years before. Meeting in Nairobi, Akeley urged him on. In his fragile state, Akeley hoped to get back to the Virungas both to complete the mountain gorilla diorama, and to keep protecting those animals still living on the mountain. More personally, he sought to experience one last time the enchantment he felt for that special place atop the mountain. To Akeley, that was the most beautiful place he had ever seen.

On October 14, before he had fully recovered his strength, the party started their long journey to the Belgian Congo, but first they would have to pass through the Uasin Gishu of western Kenya, where Akeley had once met and hunted with Theodore Roosevelt, but was now mostly wheat fields. Mary was taken aback by the two hundred "naked savages" that they would require to carry their equipage.

Reaching the Congo border, Mary noted a distinct change in the terrain. Gone were "the broad smooth footpaths of Uganda," replaced by "muddy, narrow and uneven tracks leading up and down into the depths of the jungle." The humidity was unbearable, and Mary complained that the dense vegetation gave off "unfamiliar acrid vapors in the fierce heat of noon."

Akeley advised everyone on what was really the only way to move forward. "Just put your head down and go," he said, knowing that with each step they would be ascending higher into the cooler mountain air of those foothills. It was easy enough to say, but at a steep point along the trail, Akeley collapsed. He was feeling "strange and dizzy," and Mary helped him under the shade of a tree to recover. Meanwhile, the long string of porters ahead of them continued marching on, unaware that Akeley had needed to stop. They were likely strung out along the trail for miles, given that Akeley had been lagging behind for so long. Bill ran up the trail, and after nearly two hours, returned with eight porters carrying some basic supplies and a hammock on which to transport Akeley the rest of the way.

They carried Akeley for another three miles, his body gently swaying in the hammock with each of the porters' steps, when a thunderstorm broke and forced them to stop. The terrain being too steep to make camp, they huddled under the fly of a tent to keep dry. It was clear they were never going to make it to their destination—the village just over the ridge in the next valley—and soon they would have to find a place to spend the night. A half hour later, the rain stopped and they were on the march again, certain that the main safari had already arrived in the village. Just as it was starting to get dark, they came upon some cultivated plots on a level shoulder of the mountain, and pitched Akeley's tent as another storm broke over them. Mary lay down on her cot near her husband as the thunder and lightning "crashed and flared" and the rain "fell in torrents," to the point where little streams ran under her bed.

The air cooled, and the following morning, Akeley was so refreshed he ate a hearty breakfast. "Here at last," he said, "we are on the borderland of primitive Africa." Invigorated, he walked the last three miles down a long hill into Rutshuru, where Derscheid had reserved a guesthouse. There they rested for four days while they made preparations to ascend the steep slopes of Mt. Mikeno.

Following the winding trail along the base of the mountain, Akeley was eager to find the local chief who years before had provided him with good mountain guides. But the "sultan of Burunga" had been banished from the village for murdering mail carriers and stealing their goods. Instead, the expedition pitched their tents near a rest house farther along the trail, where noisy lions kept them up part of the night as they watched the strange red glow hovering over the active volcanoes in the distance. It was enough to make Akeley get his cameras ready, expecting to get good photos as they ascended the slopes of Mikeno.

They had been traveling for nearly two weeks when they began the steady climb the next morning, and now Mary was beginning to feel a little weary, but the black slippery mud trails up the sides of Mikeno forced them all to go slow. Climbing in the cold rain, it was all very familiar to Akeley, and he pointed out the tracks of elephants and buffalo along the way.

Mary had to stop often to rest. They were gaining altitude, and the thin air sapped even the porters, crouched down along the trail as they paused briefly for a quick warming fire under the overhanging trees. The chilling rain now falling steadily, they came upon the clumps of uprooted vegetation left by feeding gorillas. "They have been here only a short time ago," Akeley said. "They may be near us even now."

When they reached Akeley's old camp at Rwero, one of Mikeno's peaks, the mist momentarily cleared, revealing the magnificent valley and Lake Kivu far below. Off in the distance, the volcanoes Karisimbi and Nyamulagira were in full view. Here amidst the swirling clouds and mists they rested, the contented Akeley smiling at the thought of finally being back.

Porters were sent ahead to establish their final base camp at Kabara, a meadow on the saddle between Mt. Mikeno and Mt. Karisimbi, but Akeley was still too ill to move, and remained at the lower Rweru Camp. On his second morning at Rweru, Akeley awoke with nausea and fever. Akeley's old gorilla tracker, Muguru, arrived to offer his services and was surprised to see how much Akeley had aged in the five years since he had last seen him on the mountain. Meanwhile, most of their supplies had already been hauled to the upper camp.

When Akeley awoke on the fourth morning, he felt much better and wanted to move to Kabara. His spirits were high. He sent for Leigh and told him to move on immediately. It was of the utmost importance to Akeley that Leigh should find the exact spot where the "Lone Male of Karisimbi" had fallen in 1921. From that precise location Akeley wanted Leigh to illustrate the panorama for the gorilla diorama background. Akeley promised Leigh that it would be a place "so fantastic and strange that you would not be surprised if you saw gnomes and fairies among the trees."

By the afternoon, Akeley was ready to move. Mary urged him to be carried in his hammock but he felt cold, and insisted on walking the last two miles to Kabara. Cold rain fell, but Akeley's spirits remained high, even when he sank up to his knees in the soft carpets of moss in those mountain cloud forests. It was good to be back. At last, he and Mary startled a group of gorillas, and when they entered the zone of the big gnarled trees, Akeley knew they were nearly there—"Here at last is where the fairies dance."

Mary was taken aback by the scene—"the abode of gnomes and fairies that Carl had called his ancient forest." She saw the enormous gnarled trees that were "decorated with flowing draperies of gray beard moss and with long trailing green vines dotted with yellow starlike flowers," and how on the massive branches of these trees were "platforms of golden green moss." From these hung "masses of fern fronds," while growing in them were "tall spikes of pink and lavender orchids." Delicate vines crept upward from the ground, "clinging to the tree trunks and covering the strangely gnarled and forked branches in . . . fragile vegetation."

Beyond beautiful, the ancient primordial site, together with the timeless presence of the mountain gorillas, evoked the deep antiquity of all ages. Akeley was sure these gorillas were his distant kin. He needed no *Dawn Man*. He only needed to capture the spirt of that elfin forest and home of the gorilla on the slopes of that ancient volcano.

The climb to their final camp had taken a lot out of Akeley. They were at eleven thousand feet, and the thin air was taking a toll on his heart. As the sun went down, the night grew colder, but Akeley did not want to retire to his tent. "No, I want to sit here," he said, before directing one of his men to set a small charcoal stove before him.

Soon Akeley was telling of the many details of how and where he had found his gorillas in 1921, as the temperature reached near freezing. He started to shiver. "Keep the lanterns burning outside the tents," he warned, thinking of the possibility of leopards in the night.

The next day Akeley made no effort to get out of bed. A runner was sent back down the trail to call for a doctor, but it would be nearly a week before one could arrive. Everyone was busy in camp, and following the instructions Akeley had given the night before, the artists went out in search of that most wonderful spot where the lone male of Karisimbi had fallen.

A storm of sleet and snow covered the ground deeply, and the air became so laden with moisture that Akeley found it hard to breathe. He felt weak but said his mind was clear. A vigil was set, and Akeley was constantly attended to as he lay in his tent, his pulse and heart rate steadily falling.

And then on the seventeenth of November, after he had been given final assurances that indeed, the artists had found his magical spot, Carl Akeley died.

EPILOGUE

A Magnificent Old Devil

"He was a magnificent old devil," the anthropologist Margaret Mead once said of Osborn. Mead had worked under Osborn at the American Museum for years, and although always a sharp critic of his racial attitudes, she nonetheless had fond memories of him. "The museum was his dream, and he built it. He was arbitrary and opinionated, but I got my first view of many things from his books and the exhibits he sponsored," Mead said. "We would have never had the museum without him."

Osborn's rise to the top of the museum's leadership had much to do with his being a member of America's ruling class. As a White Protestant man from a wealthy East Coast family, Osborn wielded immense political power, and within the museum, his formidable background in vertebrate paleontology gave him extra cachet. Andrews himself once admitted to hiding behind the meteorites just inside the Seventy-Seventh Street entrance to the museum so that he might catch a glimpse of the great Henry Fairfield Osborn strutting out to lunch. It is not surprising, then, that Osborn responded to the cultural changes taking place all around him by further romanticizing the milieu that gave him power.

Immigrants were the greatest threat to America's long-standing social order at the turn of the twentieth century. Drawn by the need for labor, these newcomers were of mostly non-Nordic ancestry—many of them Jews from Russia and eastern Europe—and they were especially inclined to settle in New York City. Their growing numbers, and differing religious and political views, challenged the cultural and political power of the ruling class. To counter this trend, Osborn turned to nature, which he believed had a moralizing effect, while at the same time he tried to bolster the aura of the White northern Europeans who first ruled the United States. Arguing that nature instilled virtues, and that human races evolved in the context of tooth-and-claw struggle, Osborn found himself promoting museum endeavors that were rooted not just in scientific inquiry but also in his quest to save the White race. Believing that evolution advanced with purpose, and seeing his own race as the pinnacle of human evolution, his quest marked the rise of scientific racism at the American Museum.

In Akeley and Andrews, Osborn found the perfect poster children for his views—men who very much captured the adventurous spirit of museum expeditions. All through the 1920s, Akeley and Andrews were in the news, and although each was driven by his individual ambitions—one to express his artistic vision with Africa Hall, and the other to gain fame as an explorer by searching for the "missing link"—both men achieved their goals by entering into a mutually dependent relationship with Osborn, who used them to perpetuate his view of an ideal American society.

Natural history is defined as the study of organisms through observation rather than experiment, and it is typically expressed through popular rather than academic outlets. It encompasses the disciplines of evolution and wildlife conservation, themes that proved especially appealing to White men struggling to define their identity and uphold their social status. The idea that a great Nordic race had evolved to represent the height of human advancement was very appealing to this demographic, who otherwise felt that they were endangered into extinction. These men stressed the importance of engaging with nature as a means of ensuring their survival, and Andrews and Akeley were among the most visible exemplars of this view.

The year 1926 was the beginning of the last chapter of Osborn's life. He would have seven more years to live, and with the Central Asiatic Expeditions uncovering so many interesting mammalian fossils—but not a single *Dawn Man*—his credibility within the scientific community wavered. Meanwhile, in another desert on another continent, an Australian anatomist named Raymond Dart had two years before uncovered an interesting primate fossil in a quarry near the South African village of Taung. The discovery of this fossil was rather nondramatic at first—there was no sweeping expedition with long lines of camel caravans, nor was there a heroic figure shooting his way past bandits—it was just Dart and his rather innocuous-looking fossil, which he put in a cigar box. But when Dart prepared this fossil, he was amazed to find the tiny skull looking human-like.

Thinking he had just discovered a new genus of human ancestor, he named the skull *Australopithecus africanus* and dated it at over a million years old. In a relatively short paper describing his discovery, Dart argued that it was not in the lush jungle lowlands that humans evolved, but rather in the harsh dry uplands that were characteristic of where he found his fossil. It was a very Osborn-like way of thinking, and indeed, Dart had found the missing link that Osborn seemed to have been looking for all along, only that Dart had found his human ancestor in the heart of Africa, and not central Asia. Dart's discovery of the Taung Child in South Africa ended the paradigm of the Asian origins of humanity, but Osborn did not even include mention of the fossil in his Hall of the Age of Man. Instead, Osborn doubled down on his idea, still believing that the evidence to support his own premise would eventually be found.

In a pivotal 1926 paper, "Why Central Asia?" Osborn launched the *Dawn Man* crusade anew, only this time he made it clear that "many decades may ensue before this prophesy is either verified or disproved." This was followed in 1927 with Osborn's most overtly romantic work–*Man Rises to Parnassus*–which reads like a novel, beginning with his *Dawn Man* and the story of how humans radiated from central Asia to seed the world with all the races imaginable. The most advanced of these, according to Osborn, were the Aryans, who migrated westward to become the Nordics. Achieving an exalted status, they developed a superior culture and society in northwestern Europe, from where they crossed the Atlantic to the New World to build, through strenuous effort, a mighty new nation called America. It was in America, according to Osborn, that all humanity reached its peak. Thus Osborn laid out his sweeping narrative of human evolution, with Osborn himself seemingly occupying the very top.

Many years after Carl Akeley's death, his good friend Roy Chapman Andrews reflected on their last encounter. Akeley was assembling equipment for his 1926 expedition when he was asked by his guide Leslie Tarleton: "Carl, do you think you are strong enough to undertake that expedition to the Congo?" As Andrews retold it, Akeley replied, "The expedition will answer that question." Knowing Akeley as he did, Andrews believed his friend wanted to die in Africa in what he believed was "the most beautiful spot in the world."

Akeley was buried near the place where he wanted to die, and it is thanks to the continued efforts of those who had worked with him–but most especially Mary Jobe Akeley–that the Akeley African Hall was finally completed as a monument to the vanishing Africa he had known and loved. Africa Hall opened on May 19, 1936, a decade after Akeley's death, but rather than being dedicated to Theodore Roosevelt, the hall is today a memorial to Akeley himself.

Roy Chapman Andrews continued the Central Asiatic Expeditions for a few more years, despite mounting political difficulties. His last expedition was in 1930, after which it was no longer possible for him to go back. His dedication to the Asiatic Expeditions ultimately cost him his marriage, but he would remarry, and when Osborn died in 1933, Andrews assumed his role as president of the American Museum. In that capacity, he was a staunch supporter of Akeley's Africa Hall, but was otherwise not as successful as Osborn, and was eventually forced out.

These were the fates of the key characters of this narrative, but what of the bigger question of their legacy? If museums are indeed artifacts of their times—synoptic displays of a society's collective hopes and fears—then what does *Palace of Deception* have to say about the times we live in today? That our most important museum collections and exhibits were built on exploitative ideas and practices is an unavoidable fact, but short of abandoning all collections as a means of making restitution, we must find some way for museums to carry on respectfully without jettisoning all the collections they have accumulated so far.

While there is a large and growing dialogue and body of published literature on the subject of museums, their troubled pasts, and how best to move forward, few touch upon the lives and ambitions of some of the historical figures who firmly believed that the work they were doing was just. Akeley and Andrews were real people who were motivated by their desire to do something great for the benefit of society, and the results of their efforts—the Akeley Hall of African Mammals and the many fossils and zoological specimens collected in Asia for the AMNH—should rightly be regarded as treasures, even though they were created within the context of a problematic past.

Carl Ethan Akeley, Roy Chapman Andrews, and Henry Fairfield Osborn were all convinced of the worthiness of their acts, but they were right only in the context of their time. If alive today, all three men would be shocked to know that their legacies are seen as perhaps something far less than righteous.

ACKNOWLEDGMENTS

I would like to thank my literary agent, Gillian MacKenzie, for her steadfast support in making this book a reality, and especially for connecting me with John Glusman, my editor at W. W. Norton. John had long before signed me for my first major work of nonfiction while he was at another publishing house, and I was thrilled to have the chance to work with him again. I would also like to thank John's editorial assistant, Wickliffe Hallos.

Colleagues at the American Museum of Natural History who welcomed me back to my former place of employment during several return visits include: Nancy Simmons, Rob Voss, Ross MacPhee, Neil Duncan, Ruth O'Leary, Elizabeth Taylor, Marisa Surovy, Eleanor Hoeger, Lauren Caspers, and John Wahlert. For providing me with hospitality while in New York, I thank my dear friends Patricia Wynne, Maceo Mitchell, and Mary Knight.

At the AMNH Gottesman Library, I was graciously received by Tom Baione, and assisted by Becca Morgan, Kendra Meyer, Greg Raml, Mai Reitmeyer, and Joel Sweimler. Kiana Clark provided access to materials in the AMNH Vertebrate Paleontology archives. I would also like to thank the staff at the Library of Congress manuscript room for making Hornaday's unpublished autobiography available. I thank

John Janelli for inviting me into his home and sharing his wealth of knowledge on museum taxidermy and Carl Akeley in particular.

As always, my longest-serving friend, and onetime scientific coauthor, Bill Schutt, encouraged me from the beginning. Bill also provided insightful commentary on several versions of the manuscript. Bill—now I owe you more than just a few favors. A special thanks also goes to my Smithsonian colleague Megan Viera for keeping me mindful of cultural sensitivities—thanks, Megan.

Finally, I would like to thank my family for their patience while I devoted so many weekends and late nights to writing yet another book—my wife, Sakiko, and our three children, Sakura, Asahi, and Midori. Persistence pays off, and while I am gratified to see another handsome book added to my shelf, I am more pleased to see how my example has influenced my daughters and son, to whom I dedicate this book. May they always work hard and see difficult tasks through to completion.

SOURCES AND NOTES

INTRODUCTION

xiii **stylish hunting jacket and pith helmet:** Regal 2002, xi.
xiii **Osborn had joined Andrews:** Osborn 1926, 266.
xiv **"Nature teaches law and order":** Haraway 1984, 20.
xiv **More immigrants arrived in America:** "Immigration," in Jackson 1995.
xiv **"insidious replacement":** Grant 1922, ix.
xiv **American Museum as a place of scientific adventure:** See Preston 1986.
xv **hundreds of scientific field expeditions:** Osborn 1911.
xvi **building my own natural history museum:** Lunde 2020.
xviii **undiminishing majesty:** See Quinn 2006.
xix **"even if the individual must suffer":** Osborn 1928, 220.
xx **"The book is my bible":** Spiro 2009, 357.
xxii **museums are treasure troves:** Johnson and Owens 2023.
xxii ***museums may be all about the past*:** Norris 2018.

CHAPTER ONE: ENTER THE KING

3 **very gracious manners:** Kennedy 1968, 114.
3 **Seventy-Seventh Street entryway:** Davey and Lesser 2019, 50.
3 **Stepping inside:** Tobin 2012, 57–60.
4 **busts of great scientists:** Osborn 1911, 33.
4 ***Jumbo* and *Samson*:** Betts 1959, 367.
4 **Albert S. Bickmore:** Rubbinaccio 2017.
4 **Louis Agassiz:** Irmscher 2013.

4 **never an orthodox churchgoer:** Irmscher 2013, 3.
5 **"so full of worthless and trashy articles":** Bell et al. 1967, 21.
5 **"made by schoolboys":** Bell et al. 1967, 22.
5 **"amuse the citizens and visitors of Washington":** Washburn 1963/1965, 106.
5 **"Without collections lectures will remain deficient":** Irmscher 2013, 111.
5 **Americans longed to be a part of something bigger:** Irmscher 2013, 108.
5 **filled the basement of Harvard Hall:** Irmscher 2013, 113.
6 **"I am looking for the professor":** Rubbinaccio 2017, 33.
6 **"you will either become utterly weary":** Rubbinaccio 2017, 33.
6 **"Professor Agassiz was as wise an instructor":** Rubbinaccio 2017, 33.
6 **"I have made some progress":** Rubbinaccio 2017, 36.
6 **each day in the museum bringing him further joy:** Rubbinaccio 2017, 36.
6 **"This work of unpacking":** Rubbinaccio 2017, 36.
6 **Bickmore decided to found his own museum:** Kennedy 1968, 30.
7 **Phineas Taylor Barnum:** Saxon 1989a.
7 ***The Happy Family*:** Saxon 1989b, 137.
7 **the showman hired Bickmore:** Rubbinaccio 2017, 42.
7 ***Feejee Mermaid*:** Kunhardt et al. 1995, 40–43.
7 ***What is it?*:** Kunhardt et al. 1995, 149.
8 **Bickmore made a detailed sketch:** Kennedy 1968, 30.
8 **Bickmore joined the Forty-Fourth Regiment:** Rubbinaccio 2017, 46.
8 **Bickmore survived fevers:** Bickmore 1869.
9 **the help of Theodore Roosevelt Sr.:** Kennedy 1968, 37.
9 **"Why cannot we now have a great popular Museum":** Davey and Lesser 2019, 23.
10 **Morris K. Jessup:** Rexer and Klein 1995, 26.
10 **move to an eighteen-acre plot:** Rubbinaccio 2017, 135.
10 **Among the earliest acquisitions:** Third and Fourth Annual Reports of AMNH (1872), 23–30.
11 **peppermint-scented oil:** Author's recollection from his time at AMNH, 1991–2010.
11 **now on display in the Smithsonian:** Rubbinaccio 2017, 141.
11 **On the first floor:** Rubbinaccio 2017, 146.
11 **illuminated every floor:** Rubbinaccio 2017, 146.
12 **almost deserted:** Kennedy 1968, 69.
12 **"No matter how fine the exhibits":** Kennedy 1968, 72–73.
12 **"check the wild extravagance":** Kennedy 1968, 76.
12 **"innocuous amusement":** Kennedy 1968, 76–77.
13 **"devotion to their work and the museum":** Kennedy 1968, 78.
13 **"We ought to have more lions":** Kennedy 1968, 79.
13 **"The resources of the Deity":** Wells 1864, 289.
14 **"aid original research":** Kennedy 1968, 92.
14 **Joel Asaph Allen:** Allen 1916.

CHAPTER TWO: PROTESTANT EVOLUTION

17 **Henry Fairfield Osborn:** Regal 2002.
17 **"We would be poor, weak, delicate plants":** Regal 2002, 31.
18 **"It is hard to believe":** Regal 2002, 31.
18 **"the child of her prayers":** Regal 2002, 34.
19 ***Harper's Weekly*:** Betts 1871.
19 **"Why can't we do something like that":** Scott 1939, 48.
20 **Their mutual hatred:** Davidson, 2002.
20 **"Well, there were before I got there":** Jaffe 2000, 198.
21 **dressed like cowboys:** Regal 2002, 41.
21 **"Our little rats of mules":** Scott 1939, 61–62.
21 **"a little felt hat":** Scott 1939, 62.
21 **"in these rocks are buried":** Regal 2002, 42.
22 **"I was leaning over my lobster":** Osborn 1924.
23 **The elder Osborn had recently acquired:** Regal 2002, 45.
24 **"write a book you cannot read!":** Regal 2002, 46.
24 **"live the same life":** Regal 2002, 47.
24 **"la Casita, in the Backstreeta":** Scott 1939, 146.
28 **"discover some new laws":** Rainger 1991, 123.
28 **"the higher ideals":** Regal 2002, 71.
28 **"the visible expression of the divine order":** Osborn 1923, 1.

CHAPTER THREE: SHOULDN'T HE BE PUT AWAY?

29 ***The Challenge*:** Akeley 1940, 38. According to the taxidermist and Akeley scholar John Janelli, the whereabouts of this early Akeley specimen are unknown (personal communication, 2023).
30 **"I can fix the canary for you":** Akeley 1941, 9.
30 **"full instructions in Skinning":** Advertisement for Sylvester's *Taxidermist's Manual* in *Youth's Companion*. Special thanks to John Janelli for making available a copy of the relevant advertisement from the January 6, 1876, issue of *Youth's Companion*.
31 **"As common things lose their charm":** Sylvester 1865.
31 **"Was he not far more than queer":** Bodry-Saunders 1991, 11.
32 ***Artistic Taxidermy in all its Branches*:** Akeley 1941, 11.
32 **Henry Ward:** Ward 1948.
32 **William T. Hornaday:** Bechtel 2012.
33 **"whacking out of the virgin jungle":** Hornaday 1938, 59.
33 **sold to Spencer Baird at the Smithsonian:** Hornaday 1938, 63.
33 **"suddenly without an instant's warning":** Hornaday 1938, 73.
34 **"with visions of my bones":** Hornaday 1938, 80.
34 **"Foolhardy at nineteen":** Hornaday 1938, 80.
35 **"land of apes and monkeys":** Hornaday 1886, 336.

36 **"The heart of Africa":** Hornaday 1886, 335.
36 **"A piece had been bitten out":** Hornaday 1886, 371.
37 **"ghastly absurdity":** Hornaday 1938, 39.
38 ***Coming to the Point*:** This diorama remains in storage at the National Museum of Natural History.
38 **"I walked all over town":** Akeley 1923, 3.
38 **"This is not a museum":** Andrei 2020, 17.
38 **"What do you want?":** Akeley 1923, 4.
39 **"characteristic attitudes":** Bodry-Saunders 1991, 19.
40 **"enough to gag a maggot":** Bodry-Saunders 1991, 25.
40 **The girl's name was Delia:** Olds 1985, 76.
41 **the Carl Akeley Company:** AMNH Mammalogy Archives, Akeley folder 1.
42 **rented from a carpentry shop:** Olds 1985, 81.
42 **chief taxidermist:** Bodry-Saunders 1991, 45.

CHAPTER FOUR: TOOTH AND CLAW

44 **Americans were fascinated with Africa:** McKinley, 1974.
44 **"They are certain, most of them":** Brinkman 2024, 7.
44 **policy of exploration:** Osborn 1911, 30.
46 **"A small party like mine":** Kirk 2010, 84.
47 **"He is a new man or ought to be":** Bodry-Saunders 1991, 50.
50 **"My communications to you":** Kirk 2010, 98.
51 **"As I advanced a few steps":** Bodry-Saunders 1991, 63–65.

CHAPTER FIVE: ELEPHANTS IN THE ROOM

54 **a lot of experimentation:** Akeley 1923, 12.
54 **"I've got it":** Bodry-Saunders 1991, 70.
54 **making artificial wax leaves:** Coleman 1922, 5.
55 **"Talk about a 'labor of love'":** Kirk 2010, 72.
56 **Word had leaked out:** Clark 1966, 14.
56 **Yale Peabody Museum:** Jaffe 2000, 367.
57 **Osborn sent Barnum to Como Bluff:** Colbert 1984, 150.
60 **"in the greater part of Africa":** Spinage 1994, 253.
60 **"In a flash I was overwhelmed":** Akeley 1933, 135.
60 **stylish wardrobe:** Olds 1985, 84.
61 **"We were going quietly":** Olds 1985, 84.
65 **looking around for another job:** Bodry-Saunders 1991, 102.
65 **communicated with Herman Bumpus in 1907:** Bodry-Saunders 1991, 105.
65 **"store bought":** Bodry-Saunders 1991, 106.
65 **"first great scheme":** Kennedy 1968, 183.
66 **"ever since he could remember":** Kennedy 1968, 182.

66 **"an inexplicable fascination with elephants":** Kennedy 1968, 182.
66 **"very unenthusiastic":** Kennedy 1968, 182.

CHAPTER SIX: BORN TO EXPLORE

67 **"more beautiful than anything of which I had dreamed":** Gallenkamp 2001, 11.
67 **"I just don't want to go":** Andrews 1943, 20.
67 **"I was born to be an explorer":** Gallenkamp 2001, 3.
68 **"private museum":** Gallenkamp 2001, 8.
68 **"the one place I would most want to work":** Gallenkamp 2001, 10.
69 **"Monty's drowning":** Gallenkamp 2001, 10.
69 **"greatly excited":** Andrews 1943, 19.
71 **"the most thrilling":** Gallenkamp 2001, 14.
71 **lived in horror of wasting time:** Andrews 1954, 163.
71 **5-dollar-a-month raise:** Andrews 1954, 163.
72 **"Get the whole thing":** Andrews 1954, 165.
74 **"It was positively indecent":** Andrews 1943, 36.
75 **"surrounded by corpses":** Andrews 1943, 44.

CHAPTER SEVEN: NUMBER NINE

76 **"I almost leaped out of my chair":** Andrews 1943, 50.
76 **made a habit of keeping a trunk packed:** Andrews 1943, 50.
77 **"tiny women and children in their charming kimonos":** Andrews 1943, 51.
77 **"belonged completely to the Orient":** Gallenkamp 2001, 24.
78 **"I don't know what I expected her to be like":** Andrews 1943, 55.
78 **Andrews could not help but feel like Robinson Crusoe:** Andrews 1954, 174.
79 **"places of pure enchantment":** Gallenkamp 2001, 28.
80 **"living in a dream world":** Gallenkamp 2001, 29.
80 **"often staying up all night":** Gallenkamp 2001, 30.
81 **"probably changed the whole course of my life":** Gallenkamp 2001, 30.
81 **"extremely susceptible to cocaine":** Gallenkamp 2001, 31.
81 **"servant girl" named Kinu:** Gallenkamp 2001, 32.
85 **"the forest became so thick":** Gallenkamp 2001, 46.

CHAPTER EIGHT: THE ROMANCE OF NATURAL HISTORY

91 **a kind of taut masculinity:** Rainger 1991, 104.
91 ***the strenuous life*:** Roosevelt 1925, 15: 267.
91 **"I wish to preach":** Roosevelt 1925, 15: 267.
92 **"We are a nation of hunters":** Dray 2018, 6–7.

93 **"the romance of natural history":** Rainger 1991, 105.
93 **the growing popularity of laboratory science:** Regal 2002, 71–73.
93 **the museum's first expedition:** Kennedy 1968, 102.
93 **"expeditions into the past":** Kennedy 1968, 125.
93 **he sketched out plans:** Randall 2022, 86.
94 **bleak Ice Age scenes:** Knight (1946) 2001.
94 **designed to nurture a reverence of nature:** Quinn 2006, 8.
95 **"If these people cannot go to the country":** Haraway 1984, 20.
96 **America's nascent wildlife conservation movement:** Reiger 2001.
96 **"No civilized nation":** Spiro 2009, 31.
96 **"A more wretched exhibition":** Spiro 2009, 35.
97 **Grant's idea was too extreme:** Spiro 2009, 31.
97 **"a despotism of the alien":** Spiro 2009, 32.
97 **"New York is now a great foreign city":** Spiro 2009, 33.
98 **now was the moment:** Spiro 2009, 35.
98 **"I congratulate you":** Spiro 2009, 36.
99 **"unbroken wilderness":** Spiro 2009, 37.
100 **"Is this the way to start a new Zoological Park?":** Spiro 2009, 40.
100 **"All the animals of North America":** Spiro 2009, 41.
100 **"degenerates" who babbled:** Spiro 2009, 44.
100 **"low-lived beasts":** Spiro 2009, 44.
101 **"representatives of all the world's races":** Spiro 2009, 44.
101 **a boy named Minik:** Harper 2000.
101 **Ota Benga:** Spiro 2009, 44.
102 **"presiding genius of the Monkey House":** Bechtel 2012, 159.
102 **"Bushman Shares a Cage":** Bechtel 2012, 160.
102 **"There was always a crowd before the cage":** Spiro 2009, 46.
103 **"the little savage":** Spiro 2009, 46.
105 **dined together about once a week:** Spiro 2009, 88.
105 **"Race denotes what a man *is*":** Spiro 2009, 94.
106 **"violent and volcanic":** Spiro 2009, 94.
106 **"The tide will rise higher":** Spiro 2009, 94.

CHAPTER NINE: A LITTLE EYE GLEAMING REVENGE

108 **"Roosevelt Museum":** Lunde 2016.
109 **new biology:** Regal 2002, 71.
112 **a standard license:** Bodry-Saunders 1991, 114.
116 **Clark got lost:** Andrews 1954, 112.
117 **"in a reckless moment":** Akeley 1933, 235.
117 **"We quenched our thirst":** Akeley 1933, 236.
118 **"merciless little eye gleaming revenge":** Bodry-Saunders 1991, 108.
119 **"Twenty primitive, superstitious men":** Akeley 1933, 242.

CHAPTER TEN: TERRA FIRMA

121 **determined to move his life in a new direction:** Andrews 1954, 195.
121 **impressive collection of whale skeletons:** Andrews 1954, 195.
121 **Terra firma was what Andrews desired:** Andrews 1929, 163.
121 **"the lure of lands":** Andrews 1929, 163.
122 **"best girl":** Letter from Andrews's agent in Yokohama dated April 17, 1913, AMNH Mammalogy Archives, R. C. Andrews folder 1-A2.
122 **abandoned any hope of finishing his doctoral degree:** Gallenkamp 2001, 55.
122 **"I have never been quite so busy":** Andrews to Conley, November 20, 1912. AMNH Mammalogy Archives.
122 **"Mammals Living and Fossil":** Andrews to Dean of Faculty, Columbia University, May 6, 1913, AMNH Mammalogy Archives.
122 **the bubbly life of New York society:** Gallenkamp 2001, 58.
123 **Yvette Borup:** Gallenkamp 2001.
123 **Roy and Yvette were married:** Gallenkamp 2001, 60.
123 **"the birthplace of primitive humans":** Andrews 1954, 195.
124 **"Cradle of Mankind":** Gallenkamp 2001, 62.
124 **"here is a region for explorers":** Osborn 1900, 568.
125 **"popping flashlight bulbs and screaming headlines":** Andrews 1943, 129.
125 **"shooting missionary":** Andrews 1943, 129.
125 **"swinging rope bridges":** Andrews 1943, 136.
125 **"for this was a zoological expedition":** Andrews 1943, 138.
126 **"other strange animals":** Andrews 1943, 140.
126 **"almost Caucasian in type":** Andrews 1943, 141.
126 **"the steaming tropics of the Burma border":** Andrews 1943, 141.
128 **"wishing desperately":** Gallenkamp 2001, 71.
128 **"sitting disconsolately at a small table":** Gallenkamp 2001, 71.
128 **"Reynolds":** Gallenkamp 2001, 72.
128 **"city of intrigue":** Gallenkamp 2001, 73.
129 **According to Andrews's biographer:** Gallenkamp 2001, 72.
129 **"cut and slashed by the knives of wind":** Andrews 1921, 3.
129 **He rented a secluded house:** Gallenkamp 2001, 75.
130 **"une belle excursion":** Andrews 1921, 45.
131 **"the place where I could stake all to lose or win on a single play":** Gallenkamp 2001, 82.

CHAPTER ELEVEN: THE GREAT RACE

135 **"The great lesson of the science of race":** Grant 1922, xix.
135 **His book was a sweeping overview:** Spiro 2009, 145.
136 **"dark Norwegians":** The author, in large part a descendant of immigrants

from southwest Norway who had emigrated a decade before Grant's book was published, recalls his grandparents jesting about how our family was composed of such "dark Norwegians."

136 **"These dark Norwegians":** Grant 1922, 211.
137 **"Moral, intellectual, and spiritual attributes":** Spiro 2009, 148.
137 **"always a blond":** Grant 1922, 206.
137 **"nomadism as well as love of war":** Grant 1922, 208–9.
137 **"the white man par excellence":** Spiro 2009, 147.
138 **"Race implies heredity":** Grant 1922, vii.
138 **"true spirit of Americanism":** Grant 1922, ix.
138 **"If I were asked":** Grant 1922, ix.
138 **end results of human evolution applied to current generations:** Grant 1922, viii.
139 **at war with entire groups:** Spiro 2009, 138.
139 **At the most basic level, scientific racism:** Spiro 2009, 138–39.
140 **"War is in the highest sense dysgenic rather than eugenic":** Grant 1922, xiii.
140 **Galton Society:** Regal 2002, 121.
140 **"this Nordic nonsense":** Spiro 2009, 297.
141 **he wrote the president of the United States:** Spiro 2009, 200.
141 **"represents a large body of Jewish immigrants":** Spiro 2009, 299.
141 **"the wretched mass of degraded human beings":** Spiro 2009, 299.
142 **"The moral principle inherent in evolution":** Clark 2008, 117.

CHAPTER TWELVE: MONKEY IN THE MIDDLE

144 **"tell the story of jungle peace":** Andrews 1954, 126.
144 **Akeley presented his idea to Osborn:** Bodry-Saunders 1991, 141.
144 **"passing a series of pictures of primeval Africa":** Bodry-Saunders 1991, 141.
145 **"preserving forever":** Bodry-Saunders 1991, 142.
145 **Having long pushed for programs:** Rainger 1991, 106.
145 **"We have been searching for years":** Bodry-Saunders 1991, 142.
145 **"African Hall would put the American Museum first":** Bodry-Saunders 1991, 142.
145 **spacious three-bedroom apartment:** Bodry-Saunders 1991, 142.
145 **"there was no movie director":** Bodry-Saunders 1991, 143–44.
146 **"undiminished interest":** Bodry-Saunders 1991, 148.
146 **"My seeming impatience":** Bodry-Saunders 1991, 148.
147 **Tanning the elephant hides:** Akeley 1941, 148.
148 **"He had no hours of play":** Andrews 1954, 118.
148 **His personal life was a train wreck:** Bodry-Saunders 1991, 152.
148 **She doted on the monkey:** Bodry-Saunders 1991, 153–55.

150 **Akeley was infuriated:** Bodry-Saunders 1991, 155.
152 **"did not and does not differ materially":** Roosevelt 1910, 2.
152 **"Africa is the only continent":** Walton 1914, 555.

CHAPTER THIRTEEN: NEW CONQUEST

154 **Entering the museum's second-floor dining hall:** This institutional knowledge was passed to the author by fellow AMNH employee Helmut Sommer, who in the early 1990s shared his recollection of how, as late as the 1950s, staff could still enjoy a meal overlooking the Seventy-Seventh Street carriageway.
154 **"Now let's have it, Roy":** Andrews 1929, 203.
155 **"We should try":** Gallenkamp, 2001, 85.
156 **"If all goes as expected":** Gallenkamp 2001, 85.
157 **"It's a great plan":** Andrews 1929, 207.
158 **"primitive man was what they wanted":** Andrews 1954, 214.
158 **"to serve your tables in the Gobi":** Gallenkamp 2001, 99.
158 **"If no position of secretary is open":** Gallenkamp 2001, 99.
158 **"I am sending my photograph":** Gallenkamp 2001, 100.
161 **"like the prehistoric monsters":** Andrews 1943, 185.
162 **"an indescribably beautiful sight":** Gallenkamp 2001, 146.
162 **"carried through life the bodily dirt":** Gallenkamp 2001, 148.
162 **"Desolate it is":** Gallenkamp 2001, 149.
163 **"one wife, one horse, one sheep and one goat":** Gallenkamp 2001, 150; Andrews et al. 1932, 97.
165 **"The persistent chill":** Gallenkamp 2001, 155.
165 **"Almost as if led by an invisible hand":** Gallenkamp 2001, 155.
165 **"It was one of the most picturesque spots":** Gallenkamp 2001, 156.

CHAPTER FOURTEEN: MURDER ON THE MOUNTAIN

167 **Doctor Savage:** Conniff 2011.
167 **unexpectedly detained:** Savage and Wyman 1847, 420.
167 **Reverend and Mrs. John L. Wilson:** Conniff 2011.
168 **"monkey-like animal":** Savage and Wyman 1847, 420.
168 **"wild men of the woods":** Savage and Wyman 1847, 426.
168 **"quite unwell":** Conniff 2011, 227.
168 **"more ferocious than the Chimpanzee":** Savage and Wyman 1847.
168 **Paul Du Chaillu:** Reel 2013.
169 **"armchair naturalist":** Reel 2013, 57.
169 **terrifying roar:** Reel 2013, 59.
170 **"Though there are sufficient points of diversity":** Reel 2013, 78.
171 ***What is It?*:** Kunhardt et al. 1995, 149.

171 **nervous and anxious:** Akeley 1923, 202.
171 **The first living gorilla:** AMNH Archives, Akeley Collection, 1977 Acc., Box 1.
171 **"extremely affectionate disposition":** AMNH Archives, Akeley Collection, 1977 Acc., Box 1.
172 **"The more I have seen":** Akeley 1923, 196.
172 **"I hope that I shall have the courage":** AMNH Archives, Akeley Collection, 1977 Acc., Box 1.
172 **"I believe that the gorilla is":** AMNH Archives, Akeley Collection, 1977 Acc., Box 1.
173 **"I look forward to the killing":** AMNH Archives, Akeley Collection, 1977 Acc., Box 1.
173 **"I cannot possibly come back":** Akeley to Mary and Herbert Bradley, February 3, 1921, AMNH Archives.
173 **"bring back stories of beautiful Africa":** Akeley to Mary and Herbert Bradley, February 3, 1921, AMNH Archives.
174 **"a single head of game":** Akeley to James Clark, September 10, 1921, AMNH Archives.
174 **"a terrible loss of time":** Akeley to George H. Sherwood, September 28, 1921, AMNH Archives.
174 **"quickened the blood":** Akeley 1923, 201.
175 **"I'll never forget it":** Akeley 1923, 203.
175 **"king's ransom":** AMNH Archives, Akeley Collection, 1977 Acc., Box 1.
175 **"lackadaisical":** AMNH Archives, Akeley Collection, 1977 Acc., Box 1.
175 **"a wonderful spot":** AMNH Archives, Akeley Collection, 1977 Acc., Box 1.
176 **"It was up to them":** AMNH Archives, Akeley Collection, 1977 Acc., Box 1.
176 **"a great black head slowly appeared":** AMNH Archives, Akeley Collection, 1977 Acc., Box 1.
178 **"There was a heartbreaking expression":** Akeley 1923, 217.

CHAPTER FIFTEEN: THE AGE OF MAN

179 **Hall of the Age of Man:** Rainger 1991, 169.
179 **seven fossil horses:** Matthew 1908.
180 **"the dominion of man":** Matthew 1908.
180 **"A race of animals may expend its energy":** Rainger 1991, 169.
181 **Casts of human fossils:** Regal 2002, 153.
181 **"it has been deemed wise":** *Natural History* (May-June 1920): 228–46.
182 **"An insatiable Wanderlust":** Clark 2008, 114.
182 **"not a gathering of cranks":** Spiro 2009, 212.
182 **"the multiplication of worthless members of society":** Spiro 2009, 212.
184 **"not more immigrants":** Regal 2002, 124.

CHAPTER SIXTEEN: THE GOBI DESERT

185 **unable to communicate:** Gallenkamp 2001, 157.
185 **"or at least ought to know":** Andrews 1943, 198.
185 **"We had made scientific history":** Andrews 1943, 198.
185 **"I must say":** Andrews 1943, 200.
185 **"written a new chapter":** Andrews 1943, 200.
185 **"It was satisfying":** Andrews 1943, 200.
186 **Andrews and Yvette settled into their new home:** Gallenkamp 2001, 111.
186 **spent the winter prospecting for fossils:** Gallenkamp 2001, 161.
186 **focused his attention on the living mammals:** Andrews 1924, 150.
187 **need for more fossil collectors:** Gallenkamp 2001, 163.
187 **Mackenzie "Mac" Young:** Gallenkamp 2001, 164.
187 **Buckshot:** Gallenkamp 2001, 165.
187 **"mass of gluelike mud":** Gallenkamp 2001, 165.
187 **two Russian cars loaded with furs:** Gallenkamp 2001, 165.
188 **"take three or four of our men":** Gallenkamp 2001, 166.
189 **"It would have been difficult to turn the car":** Gallenkamp 2001, 167–68.
190 **"their discovery in Mongolia was the fulfillment of a brilliant prediction":** Andrews 1926, 222.
190 **"a veritable titanothere mine":** Andrews 1926, 222.
190 **"a thousand shrieking demons":** Gallenkamp 2001, 170.
190 **"That finishes it":** Gallenkamp 2001, 170.
190 **"It was imperative":** Andrews 1926, 225.
191 **"If they did not reach us":** Andrews 1926, 225.
193 **"Never will I forget":** Andrews 1926, 244.
194 **Osborn was enchanted:** Gallenkamp 2001, 177–78.
194 **"The trip was perfect":** Andrews 1943, 219.
194 **"At four o'clock in the golden sunshine":** Andrews 1926, 244–45.

CHAPTER SEVENTEEN: SNAKE EYES

196 **"Dinosaur eggs":** Andrews 1943, 225.
196 **Featured in such magazines:** Gallenkamp 2001, 182.
196 **Andrews stayed at Osborn's town house:** Gallenkamp 2001, 182.
197 **Andrews realized his mistake:** Gallenkamp 2001, 183.
197 **The "Great Dinosaur Egg Auction":** Gallenkamp 2001, 182.
197 **"Up to this time":** Gallenkamp 2001, 183.
197 **"entirely legitimate":** Gallenkamp 2001, 185.
198 **"sucked orange":** Gallenkamp 2001, 185.
198 **Mongolia . . . Bolshevik ideology:** Andrews et al. 1932, 8.
199 **"insolent breed":** Andrews 1926, 250.
199 **"every Chinese caravan":** Andrews 1926, 250.

199 **orders to have Andrews shot:** Andrews 1926, 250.
199 **"I was certain that a show of force":** Andrews 1926, 251.
200 **"Tell your chief that *we* are ready to see him *now*":** Andrews 1926, 251.
200 **"How dare you ignore the passport":** Andrews 1926, 252.
201 **flashlight batteries . . . had to be bombs:** Andrews 1926, 252.
201 **they called the unknown people the Dune Dwellers:** Andrews 1943, 238.
202 **"Like a fairy city":** Gallenkamp 2001, 196.
202 **"New government regulations":** Gallenkamp 2001, 196.
202 **"All our clothes . . . were deeply buried":** Gallenkamp 2001, 197.
203 **"Peaceful enough it looked in the spring sunshine":** Gallenkamp 2001, 197.
203 **Andrews was asked to tend to some matters in the local museum:** Gallenkamp 2001, 197.
203 **"merciless searching of our persons":** Gallenkamp 2001, 197.
203 **new regulations tailored especially for Andrews's expedition:** Gallenkamp 2001, 197–98.
204 **"among the most precious":** Andrews et al. 1932, 271.
204 **"massive ramparts . . . banning us from the south":** Gallenkamp 2001, 203.
205 **"This single spot":** Gallenkamp 2001, 203.
205 **pit vipers:** Andrews 1954, 235–36.

CHAPTER EIGHTEEN: THE MOST BEAUTIFUL PLACE

208 **"Akeley will kill himself":** Andrews 1954, 137.
208 **"motion picture show":** Bodry-Saunders 1991, 209.
209 **"I'd like to see Mr. Eastman give a million dollars":** Akeley 1941, 225.
209 **"This is the most wonderful thing":** Pomeroy 1936, 9.
210 **"an everlasting monument":** Akeley 1923, 55.
210 **"Just take your rifle and ammunition":** Rockwell 1955, 206.
210 **"Yes indeed, you have to dress up to hunt in Africa":** Rockwell 1955, 206.
211 **"Today I am again preparing to enter Africa":** Akeley 1930, 1.
213 **"He had no capacity for conviviality":** Rockwell 1955, 208.
213 **"Akeley worked like a demon":** Rockwell 1955, 212.
215 **"going out on a cattle ranch and shooting down a steer":** Rockwell 1955, 221.
215 **"The bullet from your little gun":** Rockwell 1955, 223.
216 **"Nine dogs, eight shots, seven minutes":** Bodry-Saunders 1991, 242.
217 **"drawn, emaciated appearance":** Rockwell 1955, 228.
217 **"complete exhaustion from strain and overwork":** Akeley 1930, 150.
218 **"the broad smooth footpaths of Uganda":** Akeley 1941, 329.
219 **"Just put your head down":** Akeley 1941, 329.
219 **"crashed and flared":** Akeley 1941, 330.

219 **"Here at last . . . borderland of primitive Africa":** Akeley 1941, 331.
221 **"Here at last is where the fairies dance":** Akeley 1941, 338.
222 **"No, I want to sit here":** Akeley 1941, 339.

EPILOGUE: A MAGNIFICENT OLD DEVIL

223 **"He was a magnificent old devil":** Gallenkamp 2001, 40.
225 **Raymond Dart . . . *Australopithecus*:** Regal 2002, 167.
225 **Osborn launched the *Dawn Man* crusade anew:** Regal 2002, 169.

REFERENCES

Akeley, C. E. *In Brightest Africa*. Memorial edition. Doubleday, 1923.

Akeley, Delia. *Jungle Portraits*. Robert M. McBride, 1933.

Akeley, Mary L. Jobe. *Carl Akeley's Africa: The Account of the Akeley-Eastman-Pomeroy African Hall Expedition of the American Museum of Natural History*. Dodd, Mead, 1930.

Akeley, Mary L. Jobe. *The Wilderness Lives Again: Carl Akeley and the Great Adventure*. Dodd, Mead, 1940.

Allen, J. A. *Autobiographical Notes and a Bibliography of the Scientific Publications of Joel Asaph Allen*. American Museum of Natural History, 1916.

Alvey, M., T. Gnoske, and J. Janelli. "Akeley's Four Seasons: A Vision, an Obsession, and Sixteen Deer." *Natural History* (October 2021): 34–39.

Andrei, Mary Anne. *Nature's Mirror: How Taxidermists Shaped America's Natural History Museums and Saved Endangered Species*. University of Chicago Press, 2020.

Andrews, R. C. "Notes upon the External and Internal Anatomy of *Balaena glacialis* Bonn." *Bulletin of the American Museum of Natural History* 24 (1908).

Andrews, R. C. *Whale Hunting with Gun and Camera*. D. Appleton, 1916.

Andrews, R. C. *Camps and Trails in China*. D. Appleton, 1919.

Andrews, R. C. *Across Mongolian Plains*. D. Appleton, 1921.

Andrews, R. C. "Living Animals of the Gobi Desert." *Natural History* 24, no. 2 (1924): 150–59.

Andrews, R. C. *On the Trail of Ancient Man: A Narrative of the Field Work of the Central Asiatic Expeditions*. Garden City, 1926.

Andrews, R. C. *Ends of the Earth*. Garden City, 1929.

Andrews, R. C. *Beyond Adventure: The Lives of Three Explorers*. Little, Brown, 1954.

Andrews, R. C. *Under a Lucky Star*. Viking, 1943.

Andrews, R. C., W. Granger, C. H. Pope, and N. C. Nelson. *The New Conquest of Central Asia: A Narrative of the Explorations of the Central Asiatic Expeditions in Mongolia and China, 1921-1930.* American Museum of Natural History, 1932.

Bechtel, S. *Mr. Hornaday's War: How a Peculiar Victorian Zookeeper Waged a Lonely Crusade for Wildlife That Changed the World.* Beacon Press, 2012.

Bell, W. J., Jr., C. K. Shipton, J. C. Ewers, L. L. Tucker, and W. E. Washburn. Introduction by W. M. Whitehill. *A Cabinet of Curiosities.* University Press of Virginia, 1967.

Betts, C. W. "The Yale College Expedition of 1870." *Harper's Weekly*, October 1871, 663-71.

Betts, J. R. "P. T. Barnum and the Popularization of Natural History." *Journal of the History of Ideas* 20, no. 3 (1959): 353–68.

Bickmore, A. S. *Travels in the East Indian Archipelago.* D. Appleton, 1869.

Blodgett, W. T. "Report on Purchases Made in Europe for the American Museum of Natural History." In *The First Annual Report of the American Museum of Natural History* (1870).

Boas, F. "Changes in the Bodily Form of Descendants of Immigrants." *American Anthropologist* 14, no. 3 (July–September 1912): 530–62.

Bodry-Saunders, Penelope. *Carl Akeley: Africa's Collector, Africa's Savior.* Paragon, 1991.

Bowler, Peter J. *Evolution: The History of an Idea*, rev. ed. University of California Press, 1989.

Bradley, M. H. *On the Gorilla Trail.* D. Appleton, 1922.

Brinkman, D. *Now Is the Time to Collect.* University of Alabama Press, 2024.

Bucher, Henry H., Jr. "Canonization by Repetition: Paul du Chaillu in Historiography." *Revue française d'histoire d'outre-mer* 66, no. 242–243 (1979): 15–32.

Chambers, Paul. *Jumbo: This Being the True Story of the Greatest Elephant in the World.* Steerforth, 2008.

Clark, C. A. *God—or Gorilla: Images of Evolution in the Jazz Age.* Johns Hopkins University Press, 2008.

Clark, J. L. *Good Hunting. Fifty Years of Collecting and Preparing Habitat Groups for the American Museum.* University of Oklahoma Press, 1966.

Colbert, E. H. *The Great Dinosaur Hunters and Their Discoveries.* Dover, 1984.

Coleman, L. V. *Plants of Wax.* American Museum of Natural History Guide Leaflet Series, no. 54, 1922.

Conniff, Richard. *The Species Seekers: Heroes, Fools, and the Mad Pursuit of Life on Earth.* W. W. Norton, 2011.

Coon, C. S. *The Races of Europe.* Macmillan, 1939.

Davey, C., and T. A. Lesser. *The American Museum of Natural History and How It Got That Way.* Empire State Editions, 2019.

Davidson, J. "Bonehead Mistakes: The Background in Scientific Literature and Illustrations for Edward Drinker Cope's First Restoration of *Elasmosaurus platyurus*." *Proceedings of the Academy of Natural Sciences of Philadelphia* 152 (2002): 215–40.

Desalle, R., and I. Tattersall. *Understanding Race.* Cambridge University Press, 2022.

Dray, Philip. *The Fair Chase: The Epic Story of Hunting in America.* Basic, 2018.

Field Museum of Natural History. "Annual Report of the Director to the Board of Trustees for the Year 1896–97." Field Columbian Museum Pub. 24, 1897.

Gallenkamp, C. *Dragon Hunter: Roy Chapman Andrews and the Central Asiatic Expeditions.* Viking, 2001.

Grant, Madison. *The Passing of the Great Race.* Charles Scribner's Sons, 1922.

Groneman, Carol, and David M. Reimers. "Immigration." In *The Encyclopedia of New York City,* edited by Kenneth T. Jackson. Yale University Press, 1995, 181–87.

Haraway, D. "Teddy Bear Patriarchy: Taxidermy in the Garden of Eden, New York City, 1908-1936." *Social Text,* no. 11 (Winter 1984-1985): 20–64.

Harper, K. *Give Me My Father's Body: The Life of Minik, the New York Eskimo.* Steerforth, 2000.

Hellman, Geoffrey. *Bankers, Bones and Beetles: The First Century of the American Museum of Natural History.* Natural History Press, 1968.

Hornaday, W. T. *Two Years in the Jungle: The Experiences of a Hunter and Naturalist in India, Ceylon, the Malay Peninsula and Borneo.* Charles Scribner's Sons, 1886.

Hornaday, W. T. *Our Vanishing Wild Life: Its Extermination and Preservation.* New York Zoological Society, 1913.

Hornaday, W. T. *Eighty Fascinating Years: An Autobiography.* Unpublished manuscript. Library of Congress, 1938.

Hornaday, W. T. *Taxidermy and Zoological Collecting.* Charles Scribner's Sons, 1943.

Irmscher, C. *Louis Agassiz: Creator of American Science.* Houghton Mifflin Harcourt, 2013.

Jackson, K. T., ed. *The Encyclopedia of New York City.* Yale University Press, 1995.

Jaffe, M. *The Gilded Dinosaur: The Fossil War Between E. D. Cope and O. C. Marsh and the Rise of American Science.* Crown, 2000.

Johnson, K. R., and I. F. Owens. "A Global Approach for Natural History Museum Collections." *Science* 379 (2023): 1192–94.

Jonas, Louis. "The Mounting of an Elephant Group." *Publications of the American Association of Museums,* new series, no. 11, 1930.

Kennedy, J. M. "Philanthropy and Science in New York City: The American Museum of Natural History, 1868–1968." PhD diss., Yale University, 1968.

Kirk, Jay. *Kingdom Under Glass: A Tale of Obsession, Adventure, and One Man's Quest to Preserve the World's Greatest Animals.* Henry Holt, 2010.

Knight, C. R. *Life Through the Ages.* Alfred A. Knopf, 1946. Commemorative edition, Indiana University Press, 2001.

Kunhardt Jr., Philip B., Philip B., Kunhardt III, and Peter W. Kunhardt. *P. T. Barnum: America's Greatest Showman.* Alfred A. Knopf, 1995.

Lunde, D. *The Naturalist. Theodore Roosevelt: A Lifetime of Exploration, and the Triumph of American Natural History.* Crown, 2016.

Lunde, D. "Beauty and Tragedy in the Wilderness: The Naturalism of Theodore Roosevelt." In *Theodore Roosevelt: Naturalist in the Arena*. Edited by Char Miller and Clay S. Jenkinson. University of Nebraska Press, 2020.

Matthew, W. D. "Exhibit Illustrating the Evolution of the Horse." *American Museum Journal* 8, no. 8 (1908): 116–22.

Matthew, W. D. "Climate and Evolution." *Annals of the New York Academy of Sciences* 24 (1915): 171–318.

McKinley, E. H. *The Lure of Africa: American Interests in Tropical Africa, 1919–1939*. Bobbs-Merrill, 1974.

Metzler, Sally. *Theatres of Nature: Dioramas at the Field Museum*. Field Museum of Natural History, 2007.

Olds, E. F. *Women of the Four Winds*. Houghton Mifflin, 1985.

Orosz, J. J. *Curators and Culture: The Museum Movement in America, 1740–1870*. University of Alabama Press, 1990.

Osborn, H. F. "The Geological and Faunal Relations of Europe and America During the Tertiary Period and the Theory of the Successive Invasions of an African Fauna." *Science* 11, no. 276 (1900): 561–74.

Osborn, H. F. *The American Museum of Natural History: Its Origin, Its History: The Growth of Its Departments to December 31, 1909*. Irving, 1911.

Osborn, H. F. "The American Museum and Citizenship." In *Fifty-Fourth Annual Report for the Year 1922*. American Museum of Natural History, 1923.

Osborn, H. F. *Impressions of Great Naturalists: Reminiscences of Darwin, Huxley, Balfour, Cope, and Others*. Charles Scribner's Sons, 1924.

Osborn, H. F. *The Hall of the Age of Man: Guide Leaflet Series, no. 52*. American Museum of Natural History, 1925.

Osborn, H. F. *Men of the Old Stone Age*. Charles Scribner's Sons, 1925.

Osborn, H. F. "Why Central Asia?" *Natural History: The Journal of the American Museum* 26, no. 3 (1926): 266.

Osborn, H. F. *Man Rises to Parnassus*. Princeton University Press, 1927.

Osborn, H. F. *From the Greeks to Darwin: The Development of the Evolution Idea Through Twenty-Four Centuries*. Charles Scribner's Sons, 1929.

Osborn, H. F., W. B. Scott, and F. Speir Jr. "Paleontological Report of the Princeton Scientific Expedition of 1877." *Contributions from the Museum of Geology and Archaeology of Princeton College*, no. 1 (1878): 7–106.

Pomeroy, Daniel E. "Akeley's Dream Comes True: The Akeley Hall of African Mammals—a Monument to the World's Greatest Wonderland of Wild Life." In *The Complete Book of African Hall*. American Museum of Natural History, 1936.

Preston, Douglas J. *Dinosaurs in the Attic: An Excursion into the American Museum of Natural History*. St. Martin's Press, 1986.

Quinn, S. C. *Windows on Nature: The Great Habitat Dioramas of the American Museum of Natural History*. Abrams, 2006.

Rader, K. A., and V. E. M. Cain. *Life on Display: Revolutionizing U.S. Museums of Science and Natural History in the Twentieth Century*. University of Chicago Press, 2014.

Rainger, Ronald. *An Agenda for Antiquity: Henry Fairfield Osborn and Vertebrate Paleontology at the American Museum of Natural History, 1890-1935*. University of Alabama Press, 1991.

Randall, David K. *The Monster's Bones: The Discovery of T. Rex and How It Shook Our World*. W. W. Norton, 2022.

Reel, Monte. *Between Man and Beast: An Unlikely Explorer, the Evolution Debates, and the African Adventure That Took the Victorian World by Storm*. Doubleday, 2013.

Regal, Brian. *Henry Fairfield Osborn: Race and the Search for the Origins of Man*. Ashgate, 2002.

Reiger, J. F. *American Sportsmen and the Origins of Conservation*, 3rd ed. Oregon State University Press, 2001.

Rexer, L., and R. Klein. *American Museum of Natural History: 125 Years of Expedition and Discovery*. Abrams, 1995.

Rockwell, R. H. *My Way of Becoming a Hunter*. New York: W. W. Norton, 1955.

Roosevelt, Theodore. *African Game Trails: An Account of the African Wanderings of an American Hunter-Naturalist*. Syndicate, 1910.

Roosevelt, Theodore. "The Strenuous Life." In *The Works of Theodore Roosevelt, Memorial Edition*, Vol. 15, *Citizenship, Politics and the Elemental Virtues*. Charles Scribner's Sons, 1925.

Rosenzweig, R., and E. Blackmar. *The Park and the People: A History of Central Park*. Cornell University Press, 1992.

Rubbinaccio, Michael J. *Bickmore's Big Adventure: The Travels of Albert S. Bickmore and the Founding of the American Museum of Natural History in New York City*. Pescara, 2017.

Savage, T. S., and J. Wyman. "Notice of the External Characters and Habits of a New Species of Troglodytes Gorilla." *Boston Journal of Natural History* 5 (1847): 245–47.

Saxon, A. H. "P. T. Barnum and the American Museum." *Wilson Quarterly* 13, no. 4 (1989a): 130–39.

Saxon, A. H. *P. T. Barnum: The Legend and the Man*. Columbia University Press, 1989b.

Scott, William Berryman. *Some Memories of a Paleontologist*. Princeton University Press, 1939.

Spinage, C. *Elephants*. T & AD Poyser, 1994.

Spiro, Jonathan. *Defending the Master Race: Conservation, Eugenics, and the Legacy of Madison Grant*. University of Vermont Press, 2009.

Sylvester, S. H. *The Taxidermists' Manual*. Published by the author, 1865.

Tattersall, I. *Understanding Human Evolution*. Cambridge University Press, 2022.

Terrie, Philip G. *Wildlife and Wilderness: A History of Adirondack Mammals*. Purple Mountain Press, 1993.

Walton, W. "The Artist-Taxidermist and the Great African Hall of the American Museum of Natural History." *Scribner's Magazine* 56 (1914): 555–58.

Ward, R. *Henry A. Ward: Museum Builder to America.* Rochester Historical Society, 1948.

Washburn, W. E. "The Influence of the Smithsonian Institution on the Intellectual Life of Mid-Nineteenth-Century Washington." *Records of the Columbia Historical Society* 63/65 (1963/1965): 96–121.

Wells, D. A. *Annual of Scientific Discovery.* Gould and Lincoln, 1864.

INDEX